REINVENTING THE WHEEL

To Mary Beth,
Patricia A. Broderick

PATRICIA A. BRODERICK

REINVENTING THE WHEEL

HARD ROADS CAN LEAD TO BEAUTIFUL PLACES

Paul S. Bradley

Rand-Smith Books

DEDICATION

To those who are treated differently because of how they look.

ACKNOWLEDGMENTS

To all the people who believed in me, even when I didn't, thank you. To those who didn't believe in me, thank you too. You motivated me to be my best.

Special thanks to Elizabeth A. Francis, whose support of and confidence in my story made this book happen.

CONTENTS

CONTENTS

CONTENTS

FOREWORD

When I, after the demanding work of hundreds of American advocates, helped draft and sponsor the Americans with Disabilities Act (ADA) in 1990, it was precisely people like Judge Broderick I had in mind. I was intimately familiar with the obstacles presented by disability: my brother was deaf, and my nephew was paraplegic. I witnessed their cruel and painful battles against the physical and social obstacles presented by their differentness. Society tends to dismiss differently-abled people when these unseen warriors can teach us so much. This is why the passage of the ADA was so important to me, and I am proud to say it has positively changed our world.

In this memoir, Pat takes us from walking to wheeling; from thirty years before the ADA until thirty years after it became law. Her narrative illustrates exactly why this important legislation was desperately needed. Pat had to dig deep to face the many hurdles confronting her. Her grit, courage, resourcefulness, and resilience helped to overcome most of them. Thankfully, for the benefit of all of us, she successfully translated the lessons learned to her work as a federal judge in Washington, DC.

Hers is a powerful story in this age of diversity, and my friend Pat is the one to tell it. Her insights and experiences as a differently-abled person touched many raw nerves. She is a lady with exacting standards and rarely settles for less. What impresses me most is she hasn't lost humor or perspective along the way. I know you will enjoy this book as much as I did.

—*Senator Tom Harkin (retired)*

INTRODUCTION

I never thought I would write a book. Over the years people have encouraged me to do so frequently because I am supposedly such an "inspiration." That attitude has always galled me. I am just living my life like everyone else does. But there is no "ordinary" or "normal" when you are handicapped. You are either pitiful or an inspiration. So, I am sorry if that is what you are looking for, because my story isn't particularly special. At least, that is, unless you join the multitudes who think that a physically disabled person living a "normal" life is an "inspiration." But this story is not meant to be "inspiration porn." You will have to find that elsewhere, as that is not what this book provides.

My story is something we all know. It is a story of unexpected change and the power and willingness to embrace it. But in my case, it is also a story of the power of fear – the kind that can drive you forward or make you hit the brakes. It is a story of what happens when the rules don't apply to you anymore and you have to make your own rules. It is a story of rising from invisible to full living color. It is a story of what a person can become when they discard the biases and stereotypes of others and just decide to fully be themselves. It is a story of the hard fight, in current society, just to be happy in your own skin. It is a story of having the strength to face the negativity thrown at you and come out happy. It is a story about embracing your own diversity and learning to embrace it in others as well.

For all the love and support of friends and family, this would be mostly a solo trip. The decisions on how to view life and its unexpected twists and turns are always personal. But decisions must be made if one chooses to live, and to live in society. Society can be ruthless. It comes with biases, prejudices, expectations, social norms, and so much more. In these days of social media, it plunges to dazzling new depths. There are constant roadblocks thrown in the way of any attempt at an accomplishment. These are obstacles that don't need to be – biases, prejudices, and stereotypes that have no known basis in fact. Yet, unthinkingly, we accept them.

But what if we didn't? What if we challenged them? Who would we be? Who could we become? What could we accomplish? What is our unobstructed potential?

But what then? What is left? A period of gratefulness that you are still alive. A period of anger that you are still alive. A period of feeling like the Gods are deserting you. And then the realization that: You are on your own. What do you want to do?

So, the time came to chart a new course. What did I have to lose by challenging all of these expectations? What good was surviving if I couldn't do it well? When the doctor told me "Life can STILL be good," I told him that wasn't good enough. (But truthfully, at that point, even I didn't know what I meant.)

So, this is a story about the challenge. It is no picnic being paralyzed. But being paralyzed by fear is even worse. This is also my story of the constant journey through fear. This is my quest to find out who I could be. If there is courage involved, it is the courage to fail. It is the courage to face the unknown. It is the courage to not punch the last person who patted you on the head with a kindly patronizing smile when you said you were a lawyer or told you how inspiring it is to watch you put your wheelchair in your car all by yourself.

It is also a story about embracing what makes you different and about learning to love where it takes you. It is about the actual JOY of being different and loving it in yourself as well as in others. So, while the facts of my story are unique to me, this journey is not. It is a journey everyone can take. If it is a journey that interests you, then please, follow me...

FEARFUL, LOST, AND INVISIBLE

I studied the defendant, trying to gauge his demeanor as he loped toward the defense table. Even hardened criminals find it difficult to disguise their apprehension of how judicial decisions can change their world. This gentleman appeared fearful, lost, and invisible like so many who appear before me.

The Stars and Stripes with the red-and-white flag of the nation's capital hang on the wall behind the solid oak bench in my regular courtroom in Washington, DC. The overwhelming power they represent can be a daunting prospect for anyone being tried.

I gazed around the courtroom from my elevated position, dressed in the traditional black robe. A few spectators were seated in the public gallery, and everything appeared as it should be. The prosecutor and defense lawyers nodded their readiness. Yet another case in my long service as a judge was ready to start.

"Let us begin," I said.

The defendant shuffled hesitantly forward and stood unmoving, head bowed. He was small, slender, and wore standard shabby urban attire: a rumpled t-shirt and baggy, dirty jeans dangling by a miracle halfway down his hindquarters.

"This will be a guilty plea, Judge Broderick," said the court-appointed defense lawyer, standing in front of his client. "The defendant will admit guilt and accept his sentence."

The court assistant passed me the case documents. I adjusted my blue-rimmed glasses and scrutinized the papers.

According to the agreement reached by all participants, the young man would plead guilty to a charge of theft with a further similar charge being dismissed.

"The defendant entered a Dollar Store and stole a chicken wing," said the young prosecutor in his navy blue suit. He represented the people of the District of Columbia. His job was to protect citizens from alleged hardnosed criminals by taking them to court and seeking justice.

"Are you telling me?" I said, interrupting the lawyer's smooth presentation. "The Superior Court, with all its resources, is here for a stolen chicken wing?"

"Yes," replied the prosecuting and defense lawyers.

"Let me get this right," I said. "You want this man to plead guilty to theft and receive a criminal record — over a chicken wing?"

"Yes, Your Honor," said the lawyers.

"Isn't there some other option?" I said. "A diversion program, perhaps, or somewhere he can receive help?"

"Your Honor," said the prosecutor, sighing impatiently. "Diversion programs haven't been effective with this defendant. He was given community service the first time he stole a chicken wing. If he had completed this satisfactorily, his case would have been dismissed and his criminal record expunged. However, before completing his punishment, he returned to the same store and stole another chicken wing. He did it deliberately, in front of the security camera, knowing he was being taped."

"Is this true?" I said.

"Yes, Your Honor," replied the defense counsel. "However, after being arrested for the second offense, he insisted on completing the community service from the first, despite knowing the first case would no longer be dismissed."

I regarded the defendant more closely. For the first time, he looked up and returned my penetrating gaze. I observed intelligence, understanding, and a hint of defiance in his eyes.

"Did you steal the chicken wing?" I said.

"Yes," he said.

"Were you hungry?"

"Yes."

"Did you eat the chicken wing?"

"Yes."

"Are you homeless?"

"Yes."

"How old are you?"

"Twenty, Your Honor."

I glared at the prosecutor and said, "Sir, clearly, this man is not stupid. He knew he was on camera. Did it not occur to you that this might be a cry for help?"

"There are other options to stealing," said the prosecutor, straightening his back and planting his feet. "He could have asked for help."

"From whom?" I said.

"I'm sorry, Your Honor. I have no idea," said the prosecutor.

"If you, a law school graduate, don't know, why would he?"

The prosecutor shrugged.

"What is your solution?" I persisted.

"Your Honor, the State wishes to deter this defendant from becoming a serial offender. He should plead guilty and be sentenced to probation," said the prosecutor.

I paused and thought for a moment. Early in my career, I worked as a probation officer and have observed how it works. As a judge, I learned its strengths and weaknesses. Probation pro-vides the defendant with referrals, such as where to go for help. However, the referrals are only activated after the defendant has had an intake interview when he is assigned a probation officer.

"This defendant," I said, glaring at the prosecutor, "has no access to transportation, appropriate ID, or a home base for re-ceiving mail and phone calls. The probation office has no way to connect with and inform him who his assigned officer would be or how he might retrieve those referrals. If we wait for probation to help, he will simply vanish, and we will lose an opportunity to help him return to mainstream society."

I regarded the defendant, who appeared attentive.

"Have you eaten today?" I said.

"No," he said.

The prosecutor refused to consider any further diversionary opportunities and insisted on going ahead with the guilty plea. Thus, the judicial procedure progressed. When it was done, the prosecutor requested the defendant be sentenced immediately. He recommended a suspended sentence with a subsequent pro-bationary period, during which time the defendant would be able to receive the referrals.

Finally, we were at a place where I, as the judge, could utilize some discretion. I refused to sentence the defendant immediately and instead continued the sentencing hearing for three weeks later. This meant the defendant was still eligible for services from the pre-trial (versus post-trial probation) program. The pre-trial program had immediate resources available.

I ordered the pre-trial services representative to find the young man some lunch and to locate additional resources for him im-mediately before he left the courthouse. I stated that nothing would be decided on the sentencing date unless the defendant had been given the tools needed to abide by any court orders. I made it clear I expected a report on the services provided to the defendant and the progress made on his behalf.

The prosecutor appeared distressed, so I explained my reasoning. If I sentenced the defendant to immediate probation, he would be doomed to failure from the outset. First, the probation office would not be able to help him since he was homeless. Second, assuming he could find food and survive, he would still not have the resources to travel to appointments to meet his new probation officer, let alone know who or where they were based. When defendants are unable to appear for court or probation appointments or cannot be located because they are homeless, a warrant is requested for their arrest. If the police manage to locate them, they are brought before the court on additional charges for failing to appear. Along with the new charge, they could have their probation revoked and be forced to serve the original suspended sentence.

The defendant returned for sentencing three weeks later, freshly groomed and looking a lot happier. He walked straighter and prouder, wearing pressed pants and a neat polo shirt. He regarded me with a smile. In the three weeks since his last appearance, he had been connected with a service agency. They had located a distant relative willing to house him. With an address, he was able to sign up for GED classes and an apprenticeship.

He was eligible to be sentenced under the city's Youth Act. If he successfully completed probation, his criminal record would be expunged. This possibility looked realistic now that he had a home base, services, and support.

After sentencing and the next case called, the defendant followed his lawyer out of the courtroom. As he passed the bench, he stopped, looked up at me, tipped his head, and silently mouthed, "Thank you."

In the interim, I had received additional information about this defendant. Previously, he had been arrested for a botched armed street robbery, had served time in custody, and had been released. Here was a young man who knew how to rob, use a weapon, and intimidate. But in his desperation to feed himself this time, it is not what he chose to do. Instead, he put himself in front of a camera and stole a chicken wing, knowing he would be caught. He completed his community service, even though he had lost the benefit he was to receive for doing it. In other words, he took responsibility for his actions and sought help the only way he knew how.

To many people, his behavior was not a positive thing. But to me, it was a success, a wonderful example of how justice could work. We must hear people when they yell for help even if they yell in atypical ways. We need to meet them where they are, not where they should be. There is no one size fits all in justice or society. We should embrace diversity, give voices to the fearful, see and welcome those who feel lost and invisible.

From my own experiences, I know something about this.

I, too, have felt fearful, lost, and invisible.

CHAPTER

2

WANDERLUST

Long before I became a teenager, I dreamed of visiting distant lands. Not only for the pleasure of the journey itself but also to fulfill my perpetual desire to experience the world through other people's perspectives. There had to be other ways to appreciate our wonderful planet beyond the narrow mindset gleaned in my own tiny New Jersey town with a population of 13,000.

When far away from home, I felt more able to relax and enjoy life. At times, I wondered whether the desire to travel, to escape, might consume me. Worrying about how I might afford to visit the places I yearned to see evolved into an obsession. I imagined, planned, and re-planned my first overseas trip for years.

In 1962, I turned thirteen years old. An eighth-grader with dark wavy hair, crooked teeth, and freckles everywhere. My nose, inherited from my father's side of the family, protruded more than I cared for, and I was tall for my age, about five feet eight. I can't say if I was a typical teenager, but I was certainly shy and awkward. The thought of standing up and speaking in public terrified me.

I attended a Catholic grammar school. We assembled each morning in the church parking lot, lining up by class, one line for girls, another for boys, with the shortest at the front and tallest bringing up the rear. There were more girls than boys, meaning we continued after the line of boys had disappeared inside. Trailing along right at the end on our own made us tall girls even more isolated, embarrassed, and ashamed.

I was one of three kids; the middle child sandwiched between two brothers. We grew up as a close family. We had three little red rocking chairs, each with our names painted on the back. We sat and dutifully watched TV on them every evening, and especially on Saturdays for the morning cartoons.

Ours was a small but happy house. We were never far from each other, but it was comfortable and encouraged family interaction and tolerance. My stay-at-home mom and my dad maintained a unified presence — you could not play one of them against the other — and their marriage was filled with humor and love. Their shared sense of humor lasted for the full sixty-nine years of their marriage, carrying them through some dark times. They shared their humor freely. As kids, when we were sick, Dad dressed up in funny clothes, spoke with a comic accent, and appeared by our sick bed with his toolkit. Dr. Von Broderick diagnosed our problem and racked his brain to decide if a saw was needed to amputate or a hammer to knock some sense into us. We ended up laughing, even though we felt miserable.

Our property was similar to most on our tree-lined street. We lived in a safe, friendly community about ten miles west of George Washington Bridge, which connected us with New York City. It was a lovely place to live, a commuter haven with parks, a library, local police, as well as excellent schools. Our all-white neighborhood housed up-and-coming lower-middle-class families who had managed to make the move from the city to the suburbs. In the summers, a handful of professional baseball players from the

New York teams rented houses there since access to New York was easy and the neighborhoods were child-friendly. At one point, Mickey Mantle lived up the block, and Ron Hunt had a house a block away in the opposite direction. Kids played kickball and baseball when they were not involved in Little League or Scouts. They walked or rode bikes to school, the local candy shop, and about any place they wanted to go. The bus from New York City stopped two blocks away from our house, and it was not unusual to be playing in the yard and look up to see our grandfather or Uncle Ed walking down the street to visit.

We moved to this small town in New Jersey when I was about five. My dad was a flavor research chemist, and we had moved to be close to his new job located in Edgewater, New Jersey. In subsequent years he left to be a consultant and later a leader in this newly emerging field. For this, his sizeable nose was a decided asset.

He worked for well-established companies such as Lever Brothers, making flavors for their popular products, including the original Lucky Whip, one of the first whipped creams sold in an aerosol can. But he reached the point where his creativity was being stifled. Eventually, when controlling his destiny became far more appealing than another twenty years of the corporate grindstone, he decided to try working for himself as a consultant and set up shop in the basement of our three-bedroom, one-bath home.

Unusual aromas frequently wafted up from the bowels of the house as he cooked up bizarre candies, whips, and gelatins he invited us to try. School friends often inquired after the next potion. Some of the flavors he developed were decidedly unpalatable: the pistachio whipped cream was particularly awful, and once, the house reeked with a smell like shoe polish for about a week. But Dad was passionate about his work and genuinely enjoyed it, and we adored popping down to his basement domain to sniff the latest tincture and proffer our opinions.

To drum up business, Dad advertised his new flavor consultancy services in specialized professional magazines. He picked up several interesting clients, such as Oscar Mayer and Phillip Morris, but one of the most opportune for me was a gentleman from Sydney, Australia. John Bryant contacted Dad and requested that he produce a flavor that was impossible to make back then. I recall it was a simple and not unusual flavor — possibly coffee — no one had yet figured out how to produce. With his usual candor, Dad informed Mr. Bryant he wished he could assist because it could make him a millionaire, but regretfully, he would have to decline. This was precisely the answer Mr. Bryant was looking for, as the question was intended to gauge my dad's knowledge, honesty, and integrity. It was the beginning of a long professional and personal friendship. Over the decades, Mr. Bryant and my dad exchanged work ideas, family news, and visits.

Mr. Bryant visited New Jersey to personally meet and confer with Dad. He had an open, friendly face, a pencil-thin mustache, an endearing accent, and a ready smile. He was the first grown man I had seen, other than the mail carrier, who wore shorts to work. I can still picture his skinny legs and knobby knees. He was a delight when sharing meals with us, beguiling my brothers and me with fascinating outback stories and amusing anecdotes. He could tell a joke with a poker face. We liked him.

With typical big-hearted Aussie hospitality, Mr. Bryant invited us to visit him and his family Down Under. He had four kids, with two daughters around my age. I obtained their address and wrote a letter to them, and we became pen pals. Unfortunately, in 1963, the cost for our family of five to travel to the other side of the world was way beyond our means, but getting to know Mr. Bryant left me with a burning desire to meet his daughters and see my first kangaroo.

Mr. Bryant persisted with his Down Under invitations. One evening at dinner, toward the end of one of his visits, I asked, "Can we go to Australia, Dad?"

"We can't afford it, honey."

"Can I go?"

"We can't afford that either, honey."

"If I pay half, will you pay the rest?" Pause.

"Okay."

It was enough motivation for me.

For the next four years, I didn't spend a dime of money coming my way and took a stab at anything to earn extra. I babysat three days a week (for thirty-five cents an hour; fifty cents after midnight), hung wet clothes on the line for ten cents a load, and saved every cash gift. My single-minded goal was to make and save enough money for the journey to Australia.

Once Dad made the deal with me, he never wavered. He listened when I spoke of my travel dreams. He asked questions about my plans and was always quietly supportive. When I had summer jobs waitressing during high school or working at the movie theater's candy counter, he watched quietly as I put my earnings into my Australia fund. In the meantime, he kept writing to John Bryant and I to his daughter. Although I stayed focused on my goal, part of me doubted it would ever happen.

During my senior year in high school, I was dragging a bit and feeling bored. I went into the kitchen for a snack. I wasn't hungry; it was just something to do. As I sat down at the kitchen table, I was surprised to find Dad pacing up and down the room with a mysterious expression on his face. As I poured a glass of milk, I thought it unusual for him to be out of his basement office at this time of day.

"Come on, Dad," I said. "What's up?"

"Didn't we discuss Australia a while ago?"

"I thought you'd forgotten."

"How much have you saved?"

"Probably not enough."

"Think again. There's a possibility of cheap tickets, provided you fly in August. They were less expensive because it's winter Down Under. Interested?"

"Are you serious?"

"Just in case, when do you want to go?"

"August first, Dad, when else?"

A few weeks later, Dad said. "Did you see your ticket?"

"What ticket?"

"To Australia."

I shrieked.

"But, Dad," I said. "I'm supposed to pay half."

"Change of plan," said Dad, grinning. "The ticket is on me, but it's from San Francisco. Can you pay your way there?"

"No problem, I'll buy a cheap student standby ticket."

"Then it looks like you're going on your first trip."

At last, the first of what turned out to be a lifetime of wanderings was about to begin. The flight stopped in San Francisco, Honolulu, and Fiji, arriving finally in Sydney.

I spent a month in Australia, and it was heaven for me.

Mr. Bryant and his family welcomed me with open arms upon my arrival at Sydney Airport. The telegram they sent to my folks announcing my safe arrival said, "Patti, best American import ever to arrive."

They were instant family. I adored them all, especially Mrs. Bryant. She was a bundle of energy, joy, and unconventional fun and became a second mom to me. Over the years, I visited her several times, and we corresponded regularly until her death fifty years later.

I enjoyed the company of all the Bryants, of course, but on mornings when the others were studying or working, Mrs. Bryant unfurled her bun, let her hair drop to her waist, and did a jig in the living room to keep me entertained. She delighted in encouraging me to try new Aussie things, such as Passiona, a soft drink with a passionfruit flavor, then passionfruit itself, along with kiwis, fish and chips, and pavlovas. She helped me find joy and laughter in everyday things. She even laughed when I burned my bathrobe by getting too close to the space heater. No worries, mate.

The Bryants made it their business to show me everything. I woke up on my first morning to the sound of kookaburra birds laughing. It made my hair stand on end and I thought it was quite early for what sounded like a party down the block. But I learned to love the happy sound. Over the next two weeks, we toured the kangaroo park, where I hugged my first koala and learned the difference between kangaroos and wallabies. We drove out to the Blue Mountains, toured Sydney City, visited friends, and attended parties. Mrs. B. (Mrs. Bryant, also known as Momma B.) took me on shopping trips to try on kangaroo skin coats (I never could make myself buy one. I just wasn't used to spending my money), and we even did some house-hunting, as Mrs. Bryant felt they needed a larger home.

Elizabeth and Julie, the two younger Bryant daughters, and I hit it off famously. However, the family saved up the most wonderful surprise for the end of my first week. They announced we were off to spend two weeks at Hayman Island on the Great Barrier Reef.

It was 1967. In my dreams, I'd already been around the world umpteen times, but in reality, I'd been nowhere, just my hometown. In the space of one week, I'd started at JFK airport and had spent two days traveling halfway around the world. There had been moments when I had been scared to death. But the fear was tinged with excitement, and sometimes it was hard to tell which was which. I'd seen, experienced, and tasted new things, and had finally arrived at the location of my dreams. And now there was more? It was rocket fuel for my teenage soul. I was off to see one of the wonders of the world. I kept pinching myself to see if it was just another fantasy.

We flew out of Sydney to Brisbane, where the airport consisted of two hangars and a bunch of various-sized planes parked on the tarmac. Each time one took off, everyone came out of the hangars to watch. Some of the planes were tiny and, I admit, made me a tad nervous, but when we boarded a large passenger helicopter, I calmed down — well, a bit.

I was excited at the prospect of my first helicopter ride. The nearest I'd been to one was watching the news reports on the war in Vietnam, which had recently begun. As we flew northward low over the Sunshine Coast and sparkling Coral Ocean toward Australia's Whitsunday archipelago, I couldn't help but worry about our boys flying over the jungles in their Huey helicopters, risking their lives for reasons many of us didn't understand.

Hayman Island was a small resort with a large restaurant, reception area, pool, and small, rustic cabins for guests. There was a small place for late-night family dancing and fun referred to as Herman's Hideaway. Every evening there was live music and entertainment in the restaurant.

On the beach, the resort offered every type of water sport, including canoeing and catamaran rides.

Then we took a three-hour boat trip and anchored at the reef. On the way, we saw a gigantic great white shark swim by the stern of our boat. It was electrifying to watch.

I am sorry to say in this age before environmental conservation, we were permitted to explore the reef, and even walk on it. It was a stunning experience. The oyster shells were as big as suitcases. There was something new and beautiful at every step and turn. The temptation to reach out and touch everything was overwhelming. Some visitors even nicked a small souvenir of shell or coral.

Only an inch or two of the ocean washed over the top of the reef, yet every yard was a kaleidoscope of living color. It was simply extraordinary.

I was wearing a yellow frock. It had a little pocket in front where I stored my bits and pieces and things I'd picked up. I bent over to examine a shell up close and inadvertently dumped the contents of my pocket into the drink, including my camera. I, therefore, have no photos of the glorious experience, but the images remain clear in my mind.

On the boat ride back to Hayman Island, the boat stank from all the fishes and crawling creatures emerging from the shells my fellow travelers couldn't resist taking home. However, the stunning views of the Southern Cross constellation made the ride even more special. It was a spectacular experience for a teenager from the New Jersey suburbs.

After two weeks on the island, I was fitter, appropriately sunburned, happier, and more socially confident than I had ever been, but my Australian sojourn was approaching its conclusion. Down Under had been a breath of fresh air for me. It took me a while to understand the Aussie accent, but the down-home friendliness and good humor were unmistakable. People greeted me with "Gooday, Yank," in their delightful antipodean dialect. The Aussies loved the Yanks.

I was sad to think about leaving all my new friends and discoveries, but the memories of my time in that magical place remain as clear as the blue water. To visit such a wonderful country, meet such kind and loving people, and be accepted as me was a life-changing experience.

But then I had to return to reality. My temporary mental high landed with a thump as the plane hit the JFK tarmac. My high school life had been less than idyllic. In my youth, I was considered the equivalent of a nerd. At school, I was frequently called derogatory names, mocked, and bullied.

The teasing began when we moved to our house, around 1954. The local Catholic school, called St. Peter the Apostle, was located six blocks from our tiny new suburban house, so I walked to school most days. The classes had been formed during first grade and the same pupils stayed together through eighth grade. When I joined the class in second grade, I was an interloper and was never allowed to forget it.

They had already studied for and completed their First Communion — a Catholic ritual — during first grade. I had not because I hadn't made the age cut-off date at my previous school, so I had to catch up at the new school. It was bad enough being the new kid but being allowed to miss class for First Communion practice — caused some envy. It was seen as the new kid receiving special treatment. One day we had a dress rehearsal for the Communion Ceremony. For this, it was traditional to wear a white dress and veil. I was seven or eight.

Afterward, I returned to my class, which was already in progress. I entered the classroom in my white outfit, feeling special. But to my classmates, I was still this new interloper. One of the boys looked up at me and started wolf-whistling (yes, second grade). Other boys followed along until the teacher stopped them. There was some laughter from the boys and a few compliments. From the girls, there was not one single peep, and they were not smiling. An icy chill enveloped the room, and it never left.

During third grade, I was assigned to straighten out the class cloakroom after lunch. I was delighted, as at this time, we had to recite the rosary aloud, and it bored me to tears. So, with great enthusiasm, I went into the cloakroom, straightened everything moveable, and stretched it out as long as I dared. When done, I turned to reenter the classroom and spotted a classmate approaching, so I smiled and waited for her. She came right up to me, looked me in the eyes, and then gave me the quickest and strongest kick in the shins she could muster, then swiftly turned around and returned to her seat.

I was hobbled. I dropped and clutched my leg and tried not to cry. When I could stand again, I wiped my eyes and slowly went back to my seat. I needed those rosary prayers now.

When I arrived home, my mother immediately spotted the huge black-and-blue mark spreading on my leg. "What happened to your leg?" she demanded. I told her. She put me in the car immediately, drove me over to my classmate's house, and demanded to see her mother. She showed her my leg and explained what had happened. The mother called her daughter in and confronted her, and she was forced to admit she had kicked me.

I don't know what her punishment was, but she never forgot the incident.

Years later, at a Girl Scout weekend, my fellow teenage campers organized a walk into the forest and invited me along. They had previously thrown my boots in the creek and stuffed a molasses-filled sock into my sleeping bag, but naively, I was pleased to be included for a change and did not anticipate anything worse. We walked companionably for a while. Eventually, the group ended up in a clearing surrounded by trees. The organizer, my old leg-kicking friend, pointed out it was now impossible to see the path we had taken. Then she suggested it was time to act. Others appeared with ropes.

"We'll tie you up to that tree," she said with a sickening smile. "And then let you go." Well, I may have been a nerd, but I was not a fool. I instantly sized up the situation. When I broke free and ran, the girls told me I was going in the wrong direction as they chased me and tried to direct me farther into the woods. They also yelled, "Go tell your mother about this one." I made it back to the camp but was terrified for the rest of the weekend, not to mention the rest of the school year. They called me Boogie because they said I picked my nose.

The teasing, jeering, insults, and mocking continued throughout the school years. I spoke to my parents about it frequently,
and they kept telling me the girls were jealous. But it made no
sense to me. I couldn't understand why anyone would be jealous
of me. I had been beaten down to the point where I believed I was
the nerd my classmates said I was.

After so much humiliation, fear, and emotional pain, I couldn't
wait to graduate. I wanted to leave all those bullies and bad
memories behind. Meanwhile, travel was a perfect diversion, the
endless daydream, and the much-needed release from my cruel
peers. As it turns out, in some ways I should consider thank-
ing them. Inadvertently, they hardened my resolve because after
dealing with them, I thought *life should be a cinch.*

I had been writing to a Swedish girl whose charming father
had visited some neighbors of ours. I asked him if I could write to
his daughter, and he enthusiastically endorsed the idea. I began
writing to Ulla-Lisa in Sweden while in eighth grade, and I invited
her to visit. At the end of my senior year, she finally arrived, and
I took her to school. For a few days, the bullying stopped because
everyone wanted to meet my tall, blonde, beautiful Swedish
friend. It was hard when she left, but we were to have many years
of visits and an endurable, remarkable friendship for many years
to come.

My journey to Australia was immediately after Ulla-Lisa had
departed. It couldn't have come at a better time. Finally, I could
move on mentally from the degrading experiences at what was
supposed to be a religious, caring, and loving school.

My visit to the other side of the world introduced me to
far more than oddball flora and fauna or bizarre sports such as
cricket and Australian-rules football. I began to discover the real
me, free from the all-consuming nonsense of peer pressure and
social rules. But it wasn't just that, their wonderful Aussie climate

or culinary fare. The relaxed attitudes of friendly people taught me the concept of enjoying the moment.

One occurrence increased my understanding of the "No worries, mate" mentality: A guy friend walked more than a mile just to say goodbye before we drove to the airport on my homeward journey. I was shocked. I couldn't believe someone liked me enough to do such a thing.

The trip was amazing and made me hanker for more travel adventures. It was also my first taste of being liked just for being me, just me, without any need to put on airs or attempt to be cool. I loved discovering new locations and meeting new people in places where we were free to be ourselves.

THE FAMILY

My mom was a tough lady. A friend once described her as a practical mystic. She was ahead of her time in many ways and never quite figured out how to channel her energy. Looking back, I can see she was talented, smart, and strong but trapped by the attitudes of her generation. She was expected to marry and be a good wife and mother. But deep within, my mom wanted to be more of a star — better yet, the force or manager behind the star. It didn't seem to work with Dad, but she had success with me. She could push me in a direction with fun suggestions or tell me what I could never do — to make me respond out of spite. She knocked me down if I strayed but was my best friend when on the track she had chosen for me. She was a passive-aggressive force to be reckoned with.

Family lore includes some epic stories of how strong-willed Mom was. Early in their sixty-nine-year marriage, as a new mom with three small kids, she was quite busy. My dad returned from work looking forward to a clean house and dinner. There were days when his expectations were not fulfilled. Mom was not receiving the praise and empathy she craved. Now, Dad was no slouch. He worked hard, took night classes, and did all he could to provide for the family. He also helped at home. But between work, school, and commuting, he was not home to help much.

One day, Dad had had enough. He was tired of seeing the same dirty dishes still in the sink night after night. He decided to teach Mom a lesson. He told her if she didn't clean the dishes, he would throw them out. The next night, when he returned from work, the dishes were still dirty in the sink, so he did just that. But Mom didn't fold her cards. She left the dishes in the trash and took them out to the garbage to be tossed. Dad was forced to purchase new dishes.

Angry as Dad was, he also adored Mom. He admired her spunk. For example, when they were traveling near Dubrovnik, in the days when it was still Yugoslavia, Mom's love of shopping came to the fore. They were eating lunch at a local pub when a group of locals began a songfest at the back of the bar. As long as the patrons supplied the booze, the singers kept up with marvelous harmonies and tones. Dad, who was a singer himself and sang in choruses most of his adult life, was mesmerized by the spontaneous entertainment. He ordered a beer and set in for the long haul, choosing to remain for as long as the men were singing. This worked out well for Mom, who had been looking for an occasion to do some "retail therapy." Mom made her way to the local crystal shops. She purchased numerous crystal glasses and some decanters at bargain prices, only to find they could not be shipped.

Dad was irritated. He had to hand-carry several boxes of heavy crystal glasses through the airports. When their tour group arrived at the airport to fly home, their flight had been delayed due to a bad snowstorm. The delay was prolonged yet again, and the tour group inevitably became bored and frustrated. One person mentioned he had purchased several bottles of the local apple brandy and wanted to share them. Alas, he had no glasses.

"No problem," Mom announced. She opened the boxes of crystal glasses and passed them around. The entire tour group sat in the airport lounge, sipping apple brandy from crystal glasses. They were passably mellow when the ten-hour delay ended, and they could board their flight. For years, Dad couldn't tell the story without a smile and a shake of his head.

Mom and Dad met at an ice-skating rink in New York City. Dad asked her to join him on the ice when the skating was for couples only. He asked her specifically because she was the only woman wearing racing skates instead of figure skates. Dad loved to skate and even participated in some skating races, with some success. He also loved baseball. He tried out for a position as a pitcher with the New York Giants and was told to come back after the war. During my childhood, Dad always coached some baseball teams, either the Little League or the Babe Ruth League. All the kids on the team loved him, and many times in high school, a cool dude said, "Hey, I know your dad. He's great." He also did some coaching for my softball team. I was so proud of my skills until the day he gave me his honest assessment: "Honey, you play like a girl."

Dad was the oldest of four in an Irish-German family. He went to school on a scholarship, both high school and then college at Cooper Union. He was a skilled storyteller with a brilliant sense of humor. He was smart, compassionate, and claimed to be socially awkward. I think the latter self-observation was the reason he was attracted to Mom's outgoing personality. He was practical and logical and did not ever seem to panic.

One day, my paternal grandfather came on an unexpected visit. Mom told him Dad was at the ballfield, so Grandpa headed on over and sat down and watched the game. My older brother, Kevin, was playing in the right field, and Dad was one of the coaches. A ball was hit straight to Kevin. He missed it as it rolled right through his legs. It happened again. And then a third time. Good ol' Grandpa was frustrated by then, so as the ball passed unheeded through my brother's legs yet again, Grandpa let loose, yelling, "Pick it up. It ain't *shit*." My grandfather rapidly became well-known around town.

Life in River Edge, New Jersey, was all-American idyllic. Kids played softball and kickball in the streets. Everyone walked or rode their bikes to school. When the town built a swimming club, my parents were smart enough to sign up. We spent many summer hours riding our bikes to the swimming club and meeting our friends there.

My parents also encouraged us to take summer school classes. We could take extra electives we found interesting or join the summer music school program. I began my flute lessons there, my brother Kevin started on the clarinet, and we both continued playing music well into adulthood. There have been many occasions in my life when the flute was my best friend. I played sad songs when depressed and poured out my soul. Gradually, I picked up the pace and played happier music until my bad mood dissipated. Music was a lifesaver when I felt lonely. It still is.

GROWING UP

College was always on my agenda. I had already done the college search thing when my parents took me on visits to schools in which I was interested. I fell in love with the lovely campus of Trinity College, now Trinity University. It was a small school with a good academic reputation in Washington, D.C. I applied and was accepted as an Early Decision by November in my final high school senior year. It meant I could relax about my academic future and enjoy the summer.

Upon my return from Australia, I began my first year at Trinity. I brimmed with a confidence I had never experienced and lusted after yet more independence.

In the summer after my sophomore year, I took the travel plunge again.

I had an opportunity to accompany a group of fellow students to Guayaquil, Ecuador, to work with the Meals for Millions Program. It was a school project for those interested in helping others, organized under the umbrella of the Wekanduit [we-can-do-it] Club. To earn money for club missions, members of the club delivered dry-cleaning and ran a birthday cake program, contacting parents to see if they wanted to buy their child a cake and then ordering and delivering it. It was fun to bring the cakes to classmates, who sometimes screamed with delight or wept for the family they were missing.

The trip presented a way for me to get back to traveling, which didn't come for free. My parents had paid everything they could toward my expensive college. I couldn't ask them for travel money, too. I had been trying to decide what I wanted to do in life and was considering social work. One purpose for the trip, besides traveling, was to determine if working with a nonprofit and helping others might help solidify my life objectives. Hopefully, I could discover whether social work was my thing or a passing fancy. Also, I yearned to speak another language. I had been studying Spanish but needed to improve my verbal skills.

I've never wanted to be a do-gooder who worked with the needy and then returned to my comfortable home at night and forgot about them. Mrs. B. in Australia coined a phrase that stuck with me. She described certain people as "cold as charity," implying a perfunctory, unfeeling, and condescending manner in which acts of charity may be conducted. I did not want to be one of those people. I craved to earn the respect of the people in the community I served. Could I, would I like it? Ecuador would tell me.

The pre-planning of the trip turned messy and chaotic. I began to worry about what I was letting myself in for. My concerns proved justified when all the women in the group eventually dropped out. I finally received a call saying I was the only one left and, therefore, the trip had been canceled. I went up to my room and cried. But then the blossoming Broderick stubbornness bit back. I went downstairs and told my parents I wanted to go to Ecuador alone. We talked it out and agreed to telephone the program director in Ecuador, Jesse Ramirez.

Making international phone calls was a rare thing to do in 1969. After long clicks, beeps, and delays on the line, we made the connection. Mr. Ramirez was shocked to receive a long-distance phone call from New Jersey. To my relief, he agreed to pick me up at the airport, find a place for me to stay, and set me to work. He was to identify me at the airport with my bright orange suit.

My parents and I discussed the situation fully and came to an agreement. To this day, I admire their willingness to listen and consider my reasoning, even when my rationale was not the logic they employed. It must have taken them great courage to let me go. This respect became the groundwork for a true friendship with my parents in later years.

I spent eight weeks in Guayaquil. After a few days on Jesse's living room sofa bed, he thankfully found a home for me with a local family. Waking up to find dead roaches crushed under me during my sleep on Ramirez's sofa bed was not the kind of travel experience I had dreamed about. I remained hopeful about my new location.

My new home with the Orellano family was in a small compound in a graceful, white-painted house on the main street leading away from downtown. It was surrounded by a large wall, also white. The main house was on one level, small but comfortable, beautifully decorated, and easily accommodated their family of four. The family was charming, sincerely friendly, and happy to try to make sense of my broken Spanish.

At the back of the courtyard behind the house was a small garage with a long staircase leading up to a little *casita* on the second floor. Here lived Abuelita, the grandmother. Her *casita* had a small kitchen dining area and two compact bedrooms, one of which the family loaned out to me.

I don't know how old Abuelita was, but she looked about one hundred and ten. She was tiny, thin as a rail, and slightly bent over, with silver-gray hair twirled into a bun at the nape of her neck. At five foot nine, I towered over her. Abuelita cooked for me every day, including the staple black beans and rice with something at each meal. I initially felt guilty this little old woman was doing the cooking, but it became clear she loved it and relished having someone to cook for. She was a dear soul and not a bad cook, especially considering she was nearly blind. I learned quickly to check each plate before I ate to ensure it was free from ants. Once that was achieved, we had interesting chats over meals, and my Spanish improved as a result. I think we both kept each other from the throes of loneliness.

While in Ecuador, I acquired a healthy respect for crickets and cockroaches. They woke me every night with their croaking. Armed with a slipper, I tracked them down and silenced them. They were attracted to lights. On the streets, swarms of them circled streetlights in huge, tunnel-shaped waves. The insects made a loud crunching sound under the wheels of passing pickup trucks. These roaches and crickets, several inches long, could not be ignored.

I was to work with a program called Meals for Millions, whose mission was to improve the health of the *campesinos* (farmers) who lived outside the city of Guayaquil. We were to teach them how to change entrenched, unhealthy habits.

The *campesinos* lived on the banks of the river Daule. The environment was jungle-like, overgrown with trees and knee-high shrubs providing some shady respite from the stifling heat. Their housing was thatched huts, usually raised on stilts, with open cut-outs for windows. Life for *campesinos* was out in the open. They used the river water for everything — as a result, the water was contaminated, possibly poisonous. Our goal was to gently encourage them to understand the dangers of their lifestyle and adopt new methods to help them evade extreme sickness and poverty.

The *campesinos* were small in stature compared with me and deeply bronzed by constant exposure to the relentless sunshine. They were strong and hard-working, shy but friendly, and when they smiled, the radiant glow filled their entire face. Ready grins often revealed gaps where teeth were missing. A few children and some adults had swollen bellies and stick-like arms and legs — a consequence, I learned, of hunger and malnutrition I had never before witnessed.

The river was their lifeblood. They drank from it, cooked with its waters, swam in it, bathed in it, washed laundry in it, and pissed in it. The Meals for Millions staff asked *campesinos* to consider the merits of boiling the water before drinking it. The benefits seemed obvious to me, but then, it was a foreign concept to them. To encourage a more nutritious diet, the staff asked *campesinos* to plant soybeans among their other crops. Meals for Millions planned to build a medical dispensary to provide *campesinos* with a central location where they could store and sell the medications they needed.

We were welcomed into their homes/huts to sit on the floor and discuss the matter. They often smiled and laughed at how I towered over most of them; they considered me as quite an oddity and spectacle. My boss and his assistant discussed options, issues, and decisions with the *campesinos* — all in Spanish. At this point, my job was to accompany our limited staff as they accompanied the *campesinos* out to the fields, observe the work, and learn the language. The people were farmers. They cultivated crops for export and subsistence. Traditional export produce was coffee, cocoa, and bananas, along with rice, corn, and palm oil.

Despite the abject poverty and starvation, amidst the mud and suffering, kindness shone through. Every minute of every day, I experienced demonstrations of pure, simple joy.

The children beamed magnificent smiles when I approached. The adults were more reserved but still happy to see me. None seemed discontent with their lot, but they knew nothing else. One day, when we had to cross a small creek about eight feet wide, the water was too wide for me to jump across and the current too strong to risk wading. There was an animated discussion among those standing nearby, way too fast for me to understand. Finally, when they escorted me farther along the creek to a place where a tree was down and spanning the river, I worked out what they had been saying. As I stepped nervously onto the log, two men jumped into the creek, one on either side of the log, and each took one of my hands to guide me across the creek along the log. The water was waist-high on them, and it was a fierce battle against the fast-moving stream. But they smiled broadly, proud of their solution and gallantry. They were waiting for me to repeat the crossing on my return. True *caballeros*.

Using the facilities in the *campo* proved daunting. There were none. One had to seek a private place among bushes, often home to poisonous snakes. With my inherent phobia of anything serpent-shaped, I deeply appreciated this fact. On the first occasion, I needed to use the facilities, I tried to slip away from a group meeting. But one of the local men followed me to ensure my safety. I wasn't sufficiently versed in Spanish to communicate my need for privacy, so our exchange was decidedly awkward. Finally, he understood and sheepishly retired, red-faced, out of view. From that day forward, I reduced my liquid intake before going out into the fields.

In town, I was either in the program's office or at the home of the family I stayed with. Eventually, I was able to help translate some of the office documents into English for them.

I took a trip with Lautaro, one of the staffers from the program to Quito, a train ride through the mountains. It felt like a journey to a parallel universe. For ten hours, we chugged along, making regular stops. At each stop, natives bearing containers of home-cooked food leaped onto the train, scooped food onto a plate in exchange for a small fee and returned a few minutes later to retrieve their plate. It was colorful and chaotic, and there was nothing I dared to eat. But I admired their resourcefulness. I found Quito beautiful, and the historic old town area particularly enchanting.

Near the end of my Ecuador trip, with my now considerably improved Spanish, I spent a few hours alone in downtown Guayaquil, souvenir hunting. I felt independent and free. It was a day I won't forget. As I wandered down the street back to the office, a gentleman walking by whispered to nobody in particular, "*Mira, la muñeca.*" (Look at the doll.) But before I had time to swell with pride, the next gentleman to pass said, "*Mira, la grandota.*" (Look at the huge girl.) However, none of their comments were malicious: they simply stated what they saw. For the remainder of the trip, I happily considered myself as "*la muñeca grandota.*" (The huge doll.)

After Ecuador, I completed my junior year at Trinity College, an all-girls school with rigorous academics. With an enrollment of a thousand, everyone knew each other. One of the reasons I selected Trinity was I knew I could be easily distracted by young men. I figured an all-girls school was best for me to concentrate on my studies. I was also questioning the beliefs I had been brought up with and felt a Catholic college would either reinforce them or encourage me to address my doubts. Trinity was perfect. It was not a finishing school, and its philosophy encouraged its students to use their minds along with their hearts, to be strong in academics as well as character — to be the best they could be.

The education I received there served me well.

I yearned to travel again the summer after my junior year, but I needed to earn some money for college expenses and beyond. I decided to work at the Ice Cream Emporium, where I had worked previously.

The ice cream parlor was a fancy place, famous for its multiple ice cream concoctions and especially a party dish called the Kitchen Sink, which had everything in it but the proverbial. It was a marvelous marketing device. People came from all around, especially for kids' parties. Each child was given a bowl and a large spoon. The waiter served the concoction in a huge, chalice-shaped tub big enough to wash a puppy in. We filled it with all types of ice cream, sticky sauces, and loads of whipped cream with a flaming sugar cube perched on top. The waitstaff hefted it onto their shoulder and carried it in with a flourish. What the customers didn't know was whenever we made a mistake with an order, we didn't throw it away but returned it to the freezer. Soon thereafter, it sprung to a new life as part of a Kitchen Sink. Brilliant.

Life at the ice cream parlor had its challenges. It was a busy, made-to-order-service place selling ice cream and other fast food. To place customers' orders, we went to the front counter and yelled out our requests. They had to be in a specific order: larger items first, followed by smaller sundaes, plain dishes of ice cream, and then malts and sodas. There were also code words. I remember a few: A plain dish of ice cream was an *up* because the server grabbed a bowl, scooped up the ice cream, and slammed the bowl onto the counter. My personal favorite, again using the code, was a split is Flatbush on the cream, takes BS, easy spank. (Translation: A banana split with chocolate and strawberry ice cream, chocolate/brown syrup, and not too much whipped cream.) The work was hard, and the pay mainly came from tips. The hourly rate was around a dollar twenty-five. We worked long and hard, the consequence of which was that ice cream lost its allure, but only for a while.

My high school friends and I continued to hang out together, visit local bars at night, and try to meet guys. We didn't have much luck in that department, but we had fun. One of the friends

I hung out with was Jane. I've known her since we were class-mates in high school. Her family had purchased a new car, and she had taken over its use. It was a gorgeous 1969 Chevy Camaro, white, with a red pinstripe on the side and a red leather interior. We felt ultracool cruising around in it. The envious looks we garnered from the in-kids, coupled with my successful Ecuador experience, had boosted my confidence.

To make the summer more fun, I convinced my parents to allow me to test for my motorcycle license. My younger brother had purchased a small motorcycle and was preparing to take his. I arranged to accompany him and take the test, too. I had finally figured out how to press the start button without flipping the bike over, so I felt suitably ready.

I went first for the ride part of the test, with my brother watch-ing. I was the only woman on the test line. When I finished, it was his turn, so I watched him. He later told me he was going to rent me out. The test guy was so busy chatting me up during my brother's test run that he didn't see the error my brother made. We both passed.

I had a lot of fun riding around on my brother's little Honda 100cc bike, wearing cut-off jeans and a midriff blouse. Cars stopped dead to see the girl on the bike. This was 1970, after all. People rolled down their windows and yelled encouragement or asked questions as they drove slowly alongside me, their eight-track blaring, *Close to You* by the Carpenters.

It was the last summer of freedom, at least in our minds, before the long slog of education was to tie us down and then force us into full-time jobs. Jane and I decided we should take a road trip around our wonderful country to see what lay beyond New Jersey before committing our noses to the grindstone. As we talked about the idea, other friends became interested. We all required parental permission, of course, but we were passably trustworthy, so approval was granted, and we could go in Jane's family's cool car.

For me, it wasn't just a road trip. It was a coming-of-age mission. I had a wonderful family, but my mom was a great procrastinator and tended not to reassure me I could do something or nag me to make it happen. In her defense, she did not have the same goals for herself. To be more precise, she had the goals but not the perseverance to carry them through. She liked being an idea person and then supervising others through their tasks. I feared I was becoming a procrastinator like her.

One Christmas, something happened that illustrated my frustration with my mom's procrastination. The family gathered around the Christmas tree, opening gifts together. I was a young teenager at the time, typically fashion-conscious. When I ripped off the wrapping paper and ribbons from one large present, I found two bolts of fabric and a sewing pattern kit for two dresses.

"What is this?" I said, looking at my mom.

"I am going to make the dresses for you," she said.

My racing teenage hormones betrayed me, and I burst into tears.

"Why are you crying?" she asked.

"Mom," I said. "They will never be finished."

She was so furious she grabbed the package, stomped right upstairs, and began sewing. I remember my dad trying to hide his chuckle as she huffed off. He said, "You hit the target there, honey."

Mom did finish the first dress. The fate of the second bolt of fabric, however, shall remain unknown.

It was the same for my friends. We had often talked about going on adventures together, but nothing ever seemed to come to fruition, and my desire to travel loomed so large in my mind that I feared it could never be fully realized. I worried my trip to Australia had been an aberration. How many times could I count on a nice family like the Bryants to sponsor me? Would there be opportunities to earn travel money once I had to support myself? The doubts were wearing me down.

Planning this road trip with my friends distracted me from my temporary attack of negative waves and gave me something to look forward to. Hopefully, it might assuage my hunger for travel and answer my growing list of questions about my maturing self. I needed to know if I was a person of my word, one who acted on her dreams and made them a reality.

All of us wanted to test how flexible we could be. We made initial plans for a general road route, but as for housing and attractions, we were going to wing it and see where we landed. It was to be a great adventure. Four of us had committed to the trip: Jean, my best friend from elementary and high school; Jane, whose parents provided the car; Jeanne, my college roommate; and me.

The girls picked me up in the Camaro in South Carolina, where I was attending a wedding. The trip was a hodgepodge of meeting people, making new friends, seeing new sights, testing the limits of spontaneity and resourcefulness, and stretching out our small kitty of funds. Our journey took us to Georgia, Mississippi, Louisiana, Florida, Tennessee, Ohio, and all the states in between.

In Atlanta, Georgia, we ended up at a sorority house at Emory University, where we slept on the floor. We booked a tour guide from the tourist bureau and embarked on seeing the city. But we didn't feel welcome at the sorority house, so we moved on. Jean's boyfriend, who attended the U.S. Naval Academy, was stationed in Pensacola, Florida. One of his friends directed us to an apartment of girls they knew, and we camped on the floor there. We partied with lots of Navy cadets and sat on the beach at night watching the illuminated fish in the surf. Leaving Jean there with her boyfriend, we headed on to Nashville, Tennessee. There, we visited with a school chum of mine at her lakeside home. In New

Orleans, Louisiana, we inquired about lodging from the friendly woman who worked at the tourist booth. She sent us to her daughter's house — without first contacting her daughter. Her daughter had been going through a rough emotional time, and her mom thought we were just the right tonic. We knocked on the door, explained why we had come, and spent a few days sleeping on her floor. Her name was Missy, and she was gracious, funny, helpful, and delightful despite her apparent emotional pain. We loved her.

Next, we headed to Dayton, Ohio, where we stayed with a friend of Jane's brother, who let us use their living room floor and went to our first state fair. Lots of hogs and earthy perfumes.

We were now qualified to write a travel guide for floor sleeping and began to yearn for the comfort of our beds. Labor Day was looming, along with our return to school and real life. We decided to head home the next day to relax before rejoining the world.

It was to be the day my real journey began.

THE JOURNEY HOME

We packed the trunk with our small items, strapped the large suitcases to the roof rack, then purchased a box of donuts and headed east on the highway.

We'd been away for nearly two weeks, and I was more than eager to get back home. Not only for the comfort of my bed but, finally, I had a boyfriend. We met at a West Point mixer during a weekend home in New Jersey. Jim was an army cadet. We exchanged many letters but only saw each other occasionally due to our school locations and educational commitments. We shared chemistry, humor, and intelligence in our connection, and I felt like I was in a real relationship for the first time. Jim was returning from overseas the coming weekend, and I looked forward to seeing him. I was filled with excitement, planning on a little rest and looking my best.

Jane drove the car out of Ohio and through West Virginia toward Pennsylvania. Shortly before we reached the Pennsylvania state line, we switched drivers. Jeanne took the wheel, I sat in the right front passenger seat, and Jane dozed in the back.

We were happy and a bit tired, but not overly so. We felt excited about our newly discovered confidence and resourcefulness and were looking forward to how it might influence our lives.

Shortly after midday, we were heading toward Washington, Pennsylvania, on what is now Highway Seventy, a winding road with lots of construction in progress. The day was bright and sunny, but the wind was strong. The bulky items strapped to the roof made it tricky to steer the Camaro in the powerful gusts, but we felt in control of the situation.

Jeanne was driving about ten miles per hour below the speed limit. Jane was lying down in the back seat, napping. I was trying to doze.

Suddenly, Jeanne yelled, "Oh, girls, I'm so sorry."

It took me a second or two to comprehend what she was saying. I looked up and realized the car was speeding straight ahead, but the highway was curving left. At that precise moment, I recalled something I'd heard when people were in accidents. The ones who relax come out okay. I told myself, *stay cool, relax.* A second later, I thought, *Patti, you idiot, this car was about to crash. You can't relax.*

I held on as tightly as I could and braced myself.

THE ACCIDENT

The car was moving fast as we smashed down a highway mileage marker. A ditch appeared ahead of us, beyond which was the base of a steep hill. With an immense effort, Jeanne managed to jerk the wheel to the left to avoid the ditch, forcing the car out of its defiant trajectory. However, our momentum remained too great. The car hit the side of the road and went into a crazy spin on the gravel shoulder.

I recall a flashing kaleidoscope of breaking glass and blood transposed over a patchwork of dirt, gravel, and grass. When the Camaro flipped over, its roof caved in and smashed into my back.

The car finally slid to a halt. I was hanging upside down, unable to move, suspended by my seatbelt, peering out through a hole where the windscreen used to be. After a few seconds, we began to check in with one another. "Jeanne? Jane?" Jeanne had cut her ankle. Jane said she was okay; she had escaped severe injury. Sensing something bad coming, she pulled a blanket over her head and jammed herself down between the front and back seats.

Suddenly, a distant memory came rushing back to me. When I was a young girl, I sneaked into my brother's room and flicked through a book about the baseball player Roy Campanella. I read the section describing his car accident. He knew instantly something was wrong because he couldn't feel his legs anymore.

Fear enveloped me.

Within seconds of the crash, my legs looked like fat sausages trying to burst out of my cut-off jeans like tight casings. When I touched my thighs, I couldn't feel a thing.

I thought, *this will go away, won't it?*

Roy Campanella's story swirled in my head. I screamed.

"What's the matter?" said Jane.

"I'm not okay," I answered as calmly as I could. "I think I've broken my back or my neck."

A man appeared alongside me. He knelt and talked calmly through the upside-down window. By now, a crowd had gathered outside the car. A man climbed on top, reached in, released the seatbelt, and attempted to pull me out through the window. Agony shot through me. I screamed, my back hurt so much.

"Hold on a minute, buddy," someone yelled. "Wait until the cops get here."

The man straightened up and shouted back, "I *am* a cop."

The newly formed crowd soon realized they weren't going to get me out through the window.

Another man, whose name I later was told was John, had the foresight to go around to the driver's door and shut the motor off. When he returned and continued talking, I remembered an emergency first-aid lesson from my youth. I pulled off my class ring, handed it to John, and said, "Hold this, please. I'm afraid my fingers might swell."

He looked bewildered.

Looking back now, I can understand his expression. The ring was the least of my problems.

I learned later John and his wife, Mary, had been driving on the highway in the opposite direction. They were on one of their selling trips. On a whim that she was never able to explain, Mary had said to John, "You have to turn around and go in the other direction."

Because they did, they were immediately behind our car and witnessed what happened. They stopped immediately. Mary ran up the road and flagged down an ambulance on its way to another accident. Incredibly, we had help within minutes. (Later, John and Mary visited me, contacted my family, offered them their apartment to stay in, met them when they arrived, and left a bottle of my dad's favorite liquor. There are angels everywhere, even when you are not looking.)

The police and ambulance team used a crowbar and other tools to right the car and bash out the jammed door. Finally, they could carefully lift me out. I tried not to scream too much despite the pain.

The paramedics laid me on a stretcher and carried me to the ambulance. As the doors closed with a *clunk*, I experienced my first real taste of all-engulfing fear. It was not to be my last. It was September 3, 1970.

RECOVERY

While the ambulance sped along, siren blaring, my mind raced in absolute terror. My legs weren't the only part of me I couldn't feel. By the rocking and jarring, we were hitting potholes and screeching around bends, but I sensed nothing anywhere. What was wrong? Where were they taking me? To quell my fear of these unknowns, I tried to distract myself. I asked the paramedics about my friends and was told they were fine. Yet this concerned me because when actors offer similar assurances on TV shows, it often infers far worse. Consequently, I constantly yearned to see my friends and be reassured of their well-being. Furthermore, I wanted them to see me, hear me speak, and know I could still talk and laugh. If they were truly okay, I did not want them to worry or feel guilty about me.

There was another distraction I latched on to.

The two male medics were handsome and clean-cut. Just how I liked my men. One was holding my hand, the other mopping my brow. Both were concerned, so I tried to lighten the mood by saying, "Excuse me, are you married?" If you ever want to see an orderly or doctor blush, just ask them that question.

The ambulance raced straight to a community hospital in nearby Washington, Pennsylvania. The paramedics sprinted me into the emergency room. A nurse removed my cut-off jeans for x-rays to be taken with a look wavering between disgust and disapproval. I explained my legs had swollen. She appeared un-convinced.

We waited for the x-ray films for what seemed like forever. Fi-nally, an aide delivered the films, and the doctor pinned them up on a light board. After much pointing and whispered conversa-tion among the medical team, I asked what the results showed.

"They are negative," said the doctor.

"What does that mean?" I asked.

"There's nothing wrong with you," he said.

I paused for a moment in disbelief, took a deep breath, and said with all the passion I could muster, "Well, you better find something because this hurts like hell."

The doctor and nurse looked startled. After a frozen moment, they began speaking quickly in hushed tones. But not to me.

I demanded to see my friends. They were ushered in, accom-panied by loads of smiles and tears. I was so relieved.

I learned later the doctors wondered whether I was faking my pain for insurance purposes. So, they put me in an ambulance with my girlfriends for company and had me transferred to an-other hospital.

At the Montefiore Hospital in Pittsburgh, technicians took yet more x-rays. It was an excruciatingly painful experience. To obtain the best images, the technicians had to hang my head over the end of the x-ray table so my chest curved upward, enabling them to place the lens close to my neck and spine. I felt as if I were falling off the table. I screamed and attempted to explain what was happening. They informed me many x-rays were needed using this method, and I would have to get used to it.

Finally, this round of x-rays was completed.

Later, in a hospital bed, a doctor came to talk with me, accompanied by a senior nurse. He carried my films. I could tell by their facial expressions this was not going to be a frivolous conversation.

"I'm sorry to be the one to inform you," said the doctor, "but something hit your back and caused one of the vertebrae to put pressure on your spine. It caused bleeding, which was bad for the spinal cord. We need to operate to relieve the pressure."

"How bad is it?" I queried.

"It's too early to tell, and we will need to peek inside to find out more. How old are you?"

"Twenty," I said. "Why?"

"In the state of Pennsylvania," he said, "if you're under twenty-one, we can't operate without permission from your parents. Which one of them should I speak to?"

"My father," I said. "He's accustomed to tending to my cuts and bruises."

"Very well," the doctor said.

The next thing I remember was moving along a hallway lying on my stomach. I heard giggling and, with enormous strain, lifted my head and saw two nurses pulling me on a stretcher/cart.

"Hey," I said. They looked startled. I was meant to have been knocked out by a heavy sedative. "I hope you're not waiting for me to go under." They looked at me and tried to shake their heads.

"Oh, no," they said.

"Good," I said, yawning deeply. "Because I am." I couldn't hold on any longer, put my head down, and went to sleep. As I faded into oblivion, I heard them giggling.

When I woke up, it was dark and noisy.

I opened my eyes and thought, I can see, so everything will be okay. I felt calm but disoriented. Then, from somewhere, I heard a voice ask, "Is my operation over yet?"

"Yes, Pat. It's over. Go back to sleep," answered an unfamiliar voice.

"Okay, thanks," I said, feeling comforted that someone knew my name and circumstances, so I did as instructed.

I surfaced hours later to see my parents looking down at me. It made my heart hurt to see so much concern on their faces.

"How are you?" said Mom.

"I'm fine," I think I said. I can't recall the exact words, just the strength of my emotions.

"We're only allowed five minutes in intensive care," said Mom. "But we'll be back in an hour."

Then my father fainted, landing on top of me.

I freaked out. Had I caused him to have a heart attack? Maybe I'd killed him. I became hysterical as the nurses struggled to pick him up and check him over.

"He's okay," they said but insisted on dragging him away in a wheelchair for tests.

I was inconsolable.

A brief time later, Dad returned. He was walking on his own, unaccompanied by a nurse or aide, and wore a rueful smile. "I think I disappointed them by being okay," he said. "There's nothing wrong. It was just a combination of tiredness after the long journey, stress, and not eating properly."

"There's more," said Mom. "They only told your brother Bryan you'd had a bad accident and were in intensive care. We couldn't discover anything else, so we jumped in the car and drove, not knowing what we might find. Would you be dead, alive, a vegetable, or still you? It was the longest nine hours of our lives."

"We've hardly slept," said Dad.

"When we saw you looking at least half alive," said Dad, "and you recognized us, the relief was overwhelming. At least we know you are still you. We can figure out the rest."

I felt such love that day from my parents. Not only did it carry me through the darkest periods of recovery, but it also helped later when I was struggling against ignorance or intransigence, which became part of my daily life experience.

My accident touched many people. My younger brother, Bryan, is one example. Bryan and I are only fourteen months apart in age, practically Irish twins. But Bryan was the cool guy, the charmer. The family used to call him "the mayor" because he knew everyone, and everyone knew him. On the night of September 3, 1970, Bryan was home alone when the phone call from the hospital came. When my parents returned from their outing, they found Bryan in a drunken state. This had never happened. It must have been upsetting for Bryan to hear the news about me. He had never admitted he cared so much for me, but his actions demonstrated his true feelings. Later, his care for me made him a real hero in my life.

The next few days lumped together. I was aware of pain but not of what I could or couldn't do. I was completely zonked due to the medications and slept, slept, and slept. During occasional conscious moments, I relished visits from anybody who came to see me. Since I was still in intensive care, the five-minute-visit rule continued to apply.

Bryan came by about two days later with his girlfriend, Jenny. My older brother Kevin was in the military and was unable to attend. I'll never forget Bryan's face the first time he saw me. He looked destroyed, which devastated me because I had no clue how to release him from his torment.

"I want you to know it's going to be okay," I said. "And you're not to worry."

"Patti," he said, "if there is anything I can do for you, absolutely anything, you just name it."

I thought for a minute and said, "Yes, Bryan, there is. It's tough to ask, but it's enormously important to me, and I hope you don't mind because it's kind of gross."

"Anything, Patti, anything."

I wiggled my nose and said, "Could you get it right there? It's itching like crazy."

He scratched my nose for me with a big, hearty laugh and made sure he did so with each visit.

One night in the hospital, there were three cardiac arrests among patients around me. I don't know whether it was the loud noises that upset me or being close to people in their death throes. I complained, which was a sure sign I was feeling better, at least.

In any event, the nurses moved me to a side room usually reserved for quarantine cases since they didn't have any then. I even had a student nurse spend the entire day with me, talking, feeding, and comforting me. Eventually, I was well enough for my visitors to stay and chat for as long as they wanted.

Jenny had to go home and return to work, but Bryan stayed and often helped me, especially at mealtimes. My parents said after his first feeding attempt, he'd called them to say how excited he was to have done something for me. I felt closer to him than ever before.

At last, I was able to move to my own room. I was thrilled because I had been promised a telephone. I had many friends I wanted to call, and many had been trying to contact me, but in the intensive care unit, flowers and phone calls had not been permitted.

I had visions of my room being a cheery place where I'd be recovering and entertaining family and friends. Sadly, it wasn't to be.

Late one evening, an aide wheeled me in a gurney through quiet, antiseptic-smelling corridors. My new room was in an older part of the hospital; it had a telephone, but the room wasn't remotely like what I had hoped for.

It had two beds. I was put into the one farther from the door, with a window at my feet. I could see the curtains blowing gently in the breeze. It was a stinking hot night, and I relished the thought of fresh air wafting over me. I waited expectantly for the air to cool me, but I couldn't feel a damn thing. It was one of the first doses of my new reality. I could see the breeze moving the curtains. I could imagine its cooling effect, but I felt nothing.

I had a light, but it was mounted on the wall behind the bed. I couldn't turn my head enough to see it, let alone reach it. My arms were still weak, and although I could now lift them slightly, I wasn't strong enough to pull the cord to call the nurse. The solution was to wrap an extension string around the cord via bedposts and then attach it to my arm. I had to yank both my arms simultaneously to pull it. Sometimes it worked, sometimes it didn't. It made me aware of just how much strength I had lost. The frustration was hard to bear.

I received another hard dose of reality when the telephone eventually rang. The sound startled me. After the accident, loud noises made me jump out of my skin. This super-sensitive startle reflex was yet another change to adjust to.

Although the phone was only about a foot from the bed, for me, it might as well have been miles away. I couldn't turn my body, and my arms weren't strong enough to pick the thing up and hold it to my ear. When I eventually could, talking for extended periods was problematic. I tried propping the receiver against my ear with the pillow, but it kept falling out of position. Anything other than a brief chat was impossible, which was frustrating and disappointing to me.

Then reality bit hard once more. Loneliness, despair, and fear again took over my psyche. How would I live? I had no answer. Soon, my mother arrived. I was thrilled. She returned the next day and almost every day that I was there.

I continued to watch the curtains fluttering at my feet, becoming increasingly frustrated that I wasn't feeling any breeze, only stifling hospital air. I was fully awake. There was no TV to distract me, and I couldn't hold a book or magazine. Although the heat was burning, my fear was even more intense. I was alone with my thoughts, and they were moving me back into fear territory. I couldn't move, and I couldn't feel.

I tried to call the nurse but couldn't see whether the call light had worked. I had tried to get her attention when she passed the room, but I didn't know whether she had heard me or not. I tried shouting, but at this stage of recovery, my voice was too feeble to reach beyond my feet, let alone the door.

My roommate called on my behalf, but she was elderly, frail, and her vocal strength as weak as mine. Her voice didn't carry far, either. By the time the nurses finally arrived, I was hysterical. They discovered I'd developed a significant fever.

What caused it, nobody knew for sure, but it was dangerously high, and my level of stress and fear hadn't helped. Temperature control in a paraplegic person is dicey, and frequently, the ability to sweat and cool down naturally is lost or impeded. The staff took me to another room, where two nurses wiped cold alcohol on me, trying to reduce my temperature. They kindly spent the night tending to and talking to me. Their presence was soothing even though I was experiencing great pain and overwhelming heat.

I requested painkillers, even though I was nervous they might become addictive. The fear of spending the rest of my life dependent on drugs, as well as being physically impaired, gave me the strength to tolerate increased pain without reverting to medications.

On this occasion, though, I relented and demanded some relief. The nurses had to check with their bosses because there was nothing prescribed on my chart. The head nurse wasn't at all sympathetic or flexible. According to her, if it wasn't written on the chart, then I couldn't have it.

Eventually, my pathetic croaking and hysterics convinced her to call the doctor at his home. Thankfully, he prescribed painkillers, but even so, I didn't fall asleep until early in the morning. It was a long and terrible night.

When the doctor arrived the next day, he said, "How do you like your new room?"

I concede I wasn't at my most polite as I described the saga of my awful night and demanded a better room.

He was furious, not with me but with the staff.

Almost immediately, I was moved to the new wing of the building and into a bright, cheerful room with yellow walls, dark wood cabinets, and a wall-sized picture window. My bed was positioned right next to the window, and I could see the sky everywhere, not to mention a magnificent view of the rear parking lot.

The sky saved my sanity, and the vehicle-packed panorama occasionally came in handy. When my parents visited, I could see our family car, bringing a touch of home to my happy yellow room. It was a cheerful place—even the buzzer worked—and somewhere I could recuperate faster.

Frequently, new members of staff walked into my room and introduced themselves. I recall meeting the social worker. She looked at me and said, "For such a pretty girl, it's amazing nothing happened to your face."

"Now *that* we could have fixed," I chuckled. "Imagine, I could have resembled anyone I fancied."

She declined to laugh at my joke.

The following day, neither did the doctor when he said, "We have good news and bad news. You can still have children."

"Tell me the good news," I replied. He was so surprised he forgot about the bad news.

I spent, altogether, about four weeks in the hospital. For the next fortnight, we focused on recovering some of my strength, which meant I had to suffer more x-rays. Shifting my body around was irritating and uncomfortable. I continued to have the awful sensation of falling when the technician draped my neck over the edge of the table. One by one, like death by a thousand cuts, these dreadful x-ray experiences accumulated into a crescendo.

"No more x-rays," I insisted one day, bursting into tears.

The staff had been having problems with the machine and kept calling me back to repeat what we had done a few hours previously. This time, I let them have both Broderick barrels.

The x-ray department dispatched a lovely young woman to implore me to allow another attempt. After I had refused her several times, she said, "Look, I'm sorry, but if you don't come with me, I'll lose my job." Then, my mother intervened. She touched a raw nerve when she insisted that I could never live with myself if I were responsible for this young woman losing her job. Reluctantly, I agreed.

The young woman and I chatted while waiting for the capricious machine to invade my person once more. She asked me where I was going to college, what I was studying, and my reading preferences. I told her I had been trying to track down a copy of Herman Hesse's *Demian*. The story of Emil Sinclair, a young boy who struggled between two worlds: illusion and reality. She kept me talking so I could forget about my nerves. I began to realize how caring she was, which I appreciated and admired. I expressed my gratitude and mentioned I adored her beautiful earrings.

When we'd completed the x-ray session, she handed me the earrings.

"I can't take these," I said.

"I insist," she said.

I cried and reluctantly accepted them.

After our final x-ray experience together, she presented me with a personally inscribed copy of *Demian*. I can never express how grateful I was for her kindness and understanding. She made me feel I was not invisible or just another body on a cart.

My next challenge was learning to sit up. The action sounding so simple, yet it proved to be an enormous and dramatic production.

My room contained a large green armchair. It was to be my target. Transferring my body from the bed to the chair needed considerable preparation, people, and painkillers. It took four strong adults about thirty minutes to maneuver me, and they had to repeat the process when it was time to return me to bed.

Even though the exercise was incredibly painful, we successfully achieved my first chair transfer without mishap. My caregivers hadn't foreseen a problem, though: I had no balance or muscular control, so I couldn't hold myself in a seated position. Inevitably, I slowly slid out of the chair and onto the floor.

They tried strapping me in with a sheet. It prevented me from slipping down, but then I couldn't hold up my head, even though I was still wearing a neck brace.

After several more painful attempts at sitting, I began to cry at even the thought of it. Yet I knew it was something I must do. Gradually, I became smarter at managing the transfer process. When I plucked up the courage to ask for another sitting session, I first requested a painkiller, knowing it took the nurse forty-five minutes to fetch it. I needed half an hour for the painkiller to take effect, leaving enough time to organize the lifters and restraining sheet.

Slowly, sitting became easier and more rewarding, but for some unknown reason, I was becoming increasingly depressed, and despite dipping deep into my resolve, I couldn't shake off the feeling. One day, I looked at my mother and asked, "What's going on with me?"

"Do you think it might be the drugs?" she said.

"Possibly," I said. "But maybe all this is finally sinking in."

One day, I regaled some unsuspecting visitors with an awe-inspiring short speech that brought tears to their eyes. I have no recall of what I said, but I know I was brave and inspiring. After they left, I became depressed. Again, Mom said: "Do you think it might be the heavy painkillers each time you transfer to the chair?"

The next time I saw the doctor, I said, "Gee, these drugs are something."

He turned to his assistant and said, "Time to cut right down on them."

Weaning myself off wasn't easy, but in the end, I was grateful for the doctor's decision.

My parents were marvelous. I was dreadfully afraid of being alone in my hospital room, as I felt vulnerable and helpless. My mother assured me I never needed to be alone and promised to be there every day, or she arranged for someone else to be there. Her presence was particularly comforting when I was upset, tense, or depressed. She used to sit in the big green chair all night long, which was incredible to me. It had been only a week or two since my accident, but it already felt like years.

My room became jammed with get-well-soon tributes: cards, letters, and flowers. A telegram arrived from Australia, and I received a constant stream of long-distance phone calls and letters, many from people I hardly knew. Kind strangers just wanted to express their love and support. One couple dropped by because their friends had asked them to deliver some roses to me. They couldn't find roses on a Sunday, so they brought me stationery with roses printed on it. "Please don't tell him they're not real roses," they said and spent time chatting with me. Somebody else stopped by when I was in intensive care. Her sister was a neighbor and had told her to pop in if she was in the area.

I felt overwhelmed and cared for and was stunned so many people were interested in me, the high school nerd. At one point, there were so many assorted blooms that the nurses redistributed them to the lonesome elderly patients down the corridor, which warmed my heart. Each time more greenery was delivered, I cried. It made me feel so happy I couldn't stop myself. Eventually, one of the nurses told me if I cried once more, she'd take the gifts elsewhere.

The experience forced me to learn how to present a more cheerful, rather than weepy, front.

I have much to thank those nurses for. Their love and tenderness slowly nudged me back from the brink of despair. Unfortunately, I can't recall many of their names, but some of them went through some pretty bad stuff with me, especially right after the accident.

Apart from my partial paralysis, the rest of my body was also suffering. Things weren't working as they should. After two weeks, the nurses were increasingly concerned about my bloated abdomen. I kept telling anyone who cared to listen that I really wasn't that rotund but now resembled an iron lung.

The problem was nothing was moving. Those old bowels of mine must have had at least two weeks' worth stuck inside me. They were in shock and didn't know how to function properly in this paralyzed body. My roommates and their visitors were even kidding me about it. One even started calling me brown eyes because, he said, if we didn't get it out soon, it was likely to rise up to my blue eyes and turn them brown. He used to send cards addressed to Patti Brown Eyes Broderick.

The nurses assumed the card was from my boyfriend. They came into my room saying, "We know who this one is from. Who else had the cheek to call you Brown Eyes?"

My mother and I laughed heartily at the iron lung situation, but it was a severe problem. Eventually, one of the nurses had an idea, and it worked. I'll spare you the details other than to say it involved a little massage, a touch of laxative, and plastic gloves. Relief finally came. I had an amazing, deep, long sleep after that experience. But it taught me my bowels were to be a complicated project for the rest of my life.

Thinner and far more comfortable, I instantly became a less irritable and slightly nicer person. The experience cemented the growing bond between the nurses and me. They did everything they could to help while remaining friendly and kind. What I respected most was they treated me without taking away my dignity. I didn't have much dignity left at this point, but the tiny amount I hung on to was priceless. It allowed me to believe I was still a human being.

The body objects when sitting in one position for too long. As a paralyzed person, your whole body is not working properly, so healing is difficult and slow. How do you heal a sore spot when your circulation is poor? You can't feel it to know if it is getting worse, yet you need continual use of the affected area. These sores can become deep and troublesome and may require surgery. Up to now, the nurses had come in every few hours to turn me over from side to side to relieve pressure on any portion of my body to prevent the possibility of bedsores. They proposed a new option, a medication-free solution for long-term patients called a circular bed. My mother and I read the descriptive pamphlet with interest. From the pictures, the device appeared to be a circular bed sandwich, and I was to be the filling. The maintenance staff wheeled it in late one Friday afternoon.

It resembled an instrument of torture and instantly filled me with dread. The contraption consisted of two large steel circles, each padded with a slim mattress, one facing up, the other down. The idea was to trap me between the two mattresses. They worked like a clamp. After being securely strapped in, the operator turned on the motor, which rotated the bed — and little me — one hundred and eighty degrees. The uppermost mattress was then removed.

Its purpose was to take the weight off my back and sores by turning me over onto my stomach. A cut-out in the mattress for my face lets me breathe and eat.

The weekend staff had no idea how the bed was supposed to function. Unlike my mom and me, they had not read the pamphlet. The first time they sandwiched me in and tried to turn me over, they hadn't tightened the clamp enough. I began to slide out as the bed turned. I communicated my mild hysteria with a mild expletive because my mother was present. However, my fear and frustration were evident in my tone and anxiety.

Ultimately, my mother instructed the staff on how to manipulate the bed properly. Another complication was when transitioning from lying on my stomach to lying on my back, I blacked out temporarily. It was my body's reaction to being raised to an almost-standing position. The sandwich-bed experience was repeated by the night shift, who also hadn't read the operating manual.

One of the side benefits of the bed was the opportunity for a lengthy study of nurses' shoes. Lying on my chest, looking through the cut-out with the flooring as my only panorama, was a tad tedious. Eventually, I could recognize who was tending to me by their footwear. One day, it was Nurse Brown's duty to turn me over in the circular bed. Mrs. Brown was a gorgeous

African-American woman with a big heart. She was one of the staff I could recognize by her shoes. It was her turn to rotate me onto my back. Because of the blacking-out sensation, I hated the process, and I expressed my concerns to her, who understood but reassured me. She hit the button, and the rotation began. As my bed began to rise, dizziness and darkness set in.

I yelled out, "Mrs. Brown, you're turning black."

"I hope so, honey," she said and burst into a peal of laughter. I did, too.

Laughter never failed to brighten my darkness. I found I could even supply it if I tried. I loved making people smile. I hated the sad, pitiful look they gave me when first approaching. My terrible jokes often changed their expression to smiles. And then I could feel human again.

The sandwich bed experiment didn't endure. My mother's stark and forceful complaints to the doctor about the incompetence and ignorance of its workings by the staff and my torrid sensations as they turned me, had made their mark.

In the seventies, hospitals were run according to a strict set of procedures. I tried to violate most of them — not to be a nuisance, but to communicate how I felt so the staff could learn and improve my treatment. These were early days in understanding paraplegia — for them and me. For example, I suffered regularly from a high fever. To bring it down, the nurses laid me on a thermostat-controlled, ice-cold mattress. Irrespective of the fluctuations in my temperature, the rules said the mattress temperature had to remain constant. At one stage, my temperature was so high I was shaking. My mother suggested they cool the temperature further, but they refused because the rules stated otherwise, until my doctor intervened.

The most memorable aspect of my four weeks of confinement was developing a warm friendship with Dr. Yale David Koskoff, my surgeon who had been responsible for my transfer to the yellow room. Good ol' Doc visited me often in intensive care and every day afterward. I remember his genuine concern, which was visible in his sad eyes and ready smile.

Seeing no reason for formality, I had taken to greeting him with, "Hi, Doc." On one occasion, I was being transferred to the green chair and beginning to pass out as he walked in. He yelled, "Hi, Doc, hi, Doc." It made me laugh and minimized my blackout to the extent I didn't quite go all the way under. We developed this Hi, Doc routine into quite a thing. When he entered the ward, if I failed to say "Hi, Doc," he'd stand there and wait for it. Then we talked. If I was happy or down, so was he.

My parents were impressed with Dr. Koskoff. He was an extremely caring person, concerned about my future. Another of my caregivers, Dr. Lowell Lubic, failed to respond to the Hi, Doc routine, preferring to maintain some emotional distance from his patients, which I respected. Dr. Lubic enjoyed the teaching aspect of his job and was often accompanied by students or interns. They gathered around my bed while he pointed out things about me as if I weren't there. To him, I was a medical case, invisible as a person.

However, I didn't let him off lightly. I frequently interrupted his pontifications to inquire if any of his cohorts were married. It was always good for a laugh. I wasn't trying to hurt him or embarrass him; I was just reminding him I was human, not a specimen. Part of healing is emotional, and being treated like a thing did not help my psyche or favor his cause.

As I edged toward my release from the hospital, the prospect of venturing into the big, wide world with no working legs began to terrify me. My list of questions was growing longer each day, especially the sixty-four-thousand-dollar one. Could I ever walk again? My doctors adeptly avoided answering.

I discovered Hi, Doc had written a nonfiction book titled *The Dark Side of the House*. I requested a copy, which he happily inscribed and presented to me. In it, Dr. Koskoff described how he had performed a lobotomy on a chronic burglar. The burglar had volunteered for the operation to see whether it could erase his criminal tendencies. I found the book and the topic fascinating, and we talked about it. I sensed his sadness when he spoke of it.

One day, I asked him if we could talk. He drew the curtains around my bed, sat down on the mattress, and said, "My time is yours." He regarded me with intensity, and I was confident he was sincere. So, I poured out all my worries.

"Doc," I said, "I can't feel anything, yet I have a boyfriend. We haven't gone far, but the little we do involves touching each other. If I can't feel his touch, it's no pleasure for me, but when he knows I can't feel it, it's not so pleasurable for him either. Does this mean I will never feel anything ever again? And how might this affect our relationship?"

I bombarded him with questions like these until, finally, he stood up. I saw tears forming in his eyes, and he said, "Patti, honestly, I don't know. I've been doing your kind of spinal operation [a laminectomy] for over twenty years, and nobody has ever asked me before. Yet, in my heart, I know this is what patients want to know. Please, keep asking me these questions so I can learn how best to respond to you and your successors." So, I did. We talked and talked, and the conversation was honest, helpful, and reassuring. When we were done, he leaned toward me and said, "Can I give you a kiss?"

"Sure," I said.

He gave me this big, sloppy kiss on my forehead.

After that, whenever he came into the room, I said, "Hi, Doc," and when he left, I said, "Where's my kiss?"

He was cute about it. Several times, he walked in and closed the curtains with great drama. He made a ceremony of removing his glasses, handing them to his assistant, and coming to give me his fatherly kiss. It gave everyone a good laugh. I will never forget Dr. Koskoff. He left a handprint on my heart.

When the time came to leave the hospital, I was teetering between excitement and dread. I hated leaving Hi, Doc, and the familiar staff I had come to appreciate so much. But the decision was made. Relocation to a rehabilitation center now, rather than later, might enhance my chances of a significant recovery. (I hoped it also meant a better chance for me to relearn to walk, but at this point, I was afraid to ask because I knew the doctors didn't have the answer to the question.) Four weeks later, Hi, Doc approved my departure to a rehabilitation center near my family's New Jersey home.

I felt an emotional strain at leaving him and the staff, whom I now considered friends. I'd grown comfortable at the hospital and had warm feelings for Pittsburgh in general. I hoped to go back to visit someday. When my caregivers settled me into the ambulance for the ride to the airport, I felt a mix of sadness, excitement, and, once again, an overwhelming sense of fear.

WHEELS ON FIRE

A distant friend of my dad's loaned us his small private airplane. Dad rode with me in the ambulance to the airport and then joined me on the plane. I was eager to experience the flight from Pittsburgh to New Jersey in such a small aircraft. To my disappointment, after I was carried aboard and secured in a prone position, the windows were too far above me to afford a view of anything but the ceiling, diminishing my excitement.

In New Jersey, an ambulance transported me to the Kessler Institute for Rehabilitation. As we drove up the driveway, I saw the sun shining on a friendly-looking red brick building. It was perched on a hill with grand views over beautiful gardens. An awning over the front entrance looked welcoming.

I thought, *Here I will learn to walk again.* Although Dr. Lubic had said I should learn to live with what I have, Hi, Doc had suggested in about a year, my prospects for mobility would be clearer. My hopeful brain had decided if I was going to a rehabilitation center, I was going to be rehabilitated. To me, rehabilitation meant walking.

Rehab is simply a gym for the mobility-impaired. The goal is to strengthen those muscles that are still working, encourage others that might learn to work and manage what remains.

Until then, I had been the only person in my universe with a significant disability. I was about to become part of a fifty-person rehab family.

Kim jumped out of a car when a guy attacked her. She was paralyzed from the waist down.

Joe was eighteen years old, a motorcycle rider whose accident had paralyzed him from the neck down. His girlfriend visited every night and held his hand even though he couldn't feel it.

Then there was Kate. She and a friend played hooky from their jobs and were injured in a car crash. She was now a quadriplegic mom with two teenage kids and a husband.

Mr. Manly became a real friend. He was an electrical worker who had both his arms burned off. He loved LifeSaver candies, and whenever I was gifted with a few, I tried to give them to him. He explained he couldn't open the wrapper, and whenever I saw him, he asked me to open it for him. He became my mission. Little did I know I was also his.

After my accident, my injury created some limitations in the movements of my right hand. Whether they were the result of the surgery or the reach of the paralysis, we never knew. Quite frankly, at this point, the cause was not important; the impact had to be dealt with. But as a right-handed person, it certainly added to my difficulties. Mr. Smith, another patient, had noticed the injury to my right hand, so when he asked me to open the LifeSaver wrappers, he always insisted I use my right hand to do it. He updated Dad on my improvements when he visited.

Mr. Manly always tried to show humor instead of pain. One day, in an occupational therapy session, he spent an hour trying to cut a piece of white bread with a knife while using his prosthetic limbs. Frustration was all over his face, and sometimes bread flew across the room, but he kept smiling and cracking jokes. We all understood.

Mr. Smith was a machinist. He had caught one hand in a machine and tried to pull it out with the other but lost both hands at the wrist. One day in therapy, he was given a brand-new model hand that could move a bit and grasp objects. Mr. Smith tried it out gleefully, pretending he was holding a martini glass at a cocktail party. The look of wonder and amazement in his eyes spoke volumes, as did his slightly teary eyes when he had to return the hand.

Then there was a resident middle-aged man who was also a new paraplegic. He taught me how to pick up small items, such as coins, from the floor. Doing this was a real feat for me at the time. It was an important skill, as all outside calls were made on a pay phone, and I frequently dropped my coins.

We all looked out for each other and were in it together, so to speak. Our days were filled with physical therapy, occupational therapy, sometimes more physical therapy, and yet more exercises. We might have felt as if we were training for the Olympics, but in the evenings, between supper and the hour that we collapsed exhausted into bed, we had plenty of time to wrestle with our inner turmoil. We got to know each other's stories. Soon, we also knew the families who visited regularly. Patients conferred with each other, and parents conferred with each other. We were in our insulated world and were temporarily safe.

The facility had a large physical therapy room where we could see each other working out. On many occasions, I was strapped to a tilt table. It held me in a vertical position to stimulate circulation and put weight on my bones. In this orientation, I could observe everyone, and folks stopped by for a chat.

A young man who suffered a stroke at the beginning of his second semester in his senior year of college could barely speak.

Focusing his eyes was also difficult. He spent hours in the library figuring out what was wrong and how to get better.

A young mother had suffered a stroke following childbirth. She could use only one side of her body and suffered from speech and focus limitations. To propel her wheelchair, she pulled with her good leg and pushed the wheel with her good arm. One day, she stopped her chair alongside mine, looked at me with a beatific smile, and said, "God is good," then wheeled away.

Thursdays were the weekly amputee clinic, where patients were assessed for suitable prosthetics and what healing to limbs would be necessary before prosthetics could be fitted. Mr. Smith and Mr. Manly were attending the clinic when a new patient wheeled up to join them. He was a nice-looking young man in his late twenties with clear, smooth skin, dark hair, and sporting a mustache. He was slim and fit but hung his head as he was wheeled up to the amputee clinic door. He had been a technician on telephone poles and had lost both legs, one below and one above the knee. Unsurprisingly, he was discouraged and disconsolate. Mr. Manly flashed him one of his wide southern smiles and, in his long Tennessee tones, said to the young man, "Well, son, how tall do you want to be?" It broke the ice, and everyone laughed. Who else but a man with no hands could ask such a question?

In early March 1971, during an occupational therapy session, I was assigned to work with a typewriter to improve my damaged right hand. I could not grip properly, and originally, I couldn't even hold a pen or pencil. It was difficult to fasten buttons or zippers and almost impossible to hold anything weighty. The middle fingers on the right hand did not work well independently, and my therapist hoped typing might strengthen them. I found typing to be frustrating and boring and practiced aimlessly since it didn't feel as if it was helping much. I assumed I had been given busy work, as if I were a bothersome kid, to keep me occupied. But over time, typing became less awkward, and I realized I could do it, though somewhat laboriously. I decided to type my thoughts. I took a minute to focus and block out the noise in the room. Then I let it rip. My thoughts and feelings just started flowing. They came out like this:

I wish there was someplace I could go
Someone I could tell
About how I want so very much
To run around in blue jeans this summer
And be part of the crowd
To be normal
Do normal things
Like splashing in the rain
Riding my motorcycle
Making guys stare
Being REAL
A girl and ALIVE
Instead of being half-dead
Where even spontaneity is something planned.

Always worrying about steps
The ocean I will never feel
The grass where I can't run or roll
Going to bars where my friends don't know what to say to me
The simple things
Gone
Because having free will and being human, I made a choice
Gone because that which makes life beautiful can also take it away
I want to cry
But I'm tired of that
It does nothing
I'm reminded to make the best of things

As if there is any choice

I crave love now
It must be the answer
A nice, strong guy
To take me to those places I can't go alone
And
He'd do it because he loved me

OK, so I'm not a poet but when I read it again, all these years later, it reminds me of the fear and melancholy I suffered during rehab. But typing my thoughts was therapeutic. It helped me cope with the reality of what I would be facing every day for the rest of my life.

The poem was just the beginning of my writing therapy. It inspired me to note everything down in a private journal. The pages were packed with errors and nonsense grammar. But the meaning of what I was trying to convey was clear. The words expressed my pain and loss as a twenty-year-old girl in a chair. Reading them again all these years later, as I write this book, has again been most therapeutic.

We held informal competitions in rehab. The competitions weren't officially on the agenda, but the aides and nurses were tolerant of our antics. We may have been impaired people, but instinctively we knew taking part in such silliness was bonding, helping the healing process, good exercise, and, more importantly, it was fun.

Everyone was determined to win the wheelchair race. And we all cheated like hell to make sure we did.

The funniest competition, though, was to see who could swallow the most pills at one time and then keep them down. Those who had been prescribed more pills had an obvious advantage —

at least in this competition. The staff was unwilling to give the rest of us additional medications so we could win the challenge.

Sometimes, the facility offered too much closeness and not enough privacy. For example, the nurse might yell at full volume, down the hall, "Has so-and-so finished their business yet?" There was no place to hide or the ability to duck. Privacy and dignity were unintentionally, but easily, abused.

Janet, one of my roommates, was a gentle woman with a doting husband. She was about forty-five years old, and her kids were grown up. She had multiple sclerosis (MS) and was going through a bad period of recession. She had lost the ability to walk, and her remaining balance was poor. Her husband visited every night to encourage her. He adored her, and she put on a brave face for him. But after he had gone home, she told me how lucky I was. She pointed out that my injury wouldn't worsen, while every morning, she wondered what ability she had lost since the previous day. One day, the feeling in her hands was gone. She couldn't tell if her pants were in her hands when she was pulling them up.

She worried constantly about finding wheelchair-accessible bathrooms and advised me Exxon gas stations had the biggest bathrooms. Whenever she traveled, it was only via Exxon routes.

It was challenging work, but slowly, I became proficient at my new skillset. Now, I could propel the chair, transfer onto the bed, enter a car, and drive it with hand controls.

This latest skill was exciting and gave me great hope. The rehab center offered driving lessons. A local gentleman was brave enough to teach us. Fortunately for him, he had a brake on his side of the car.

The rehab center used an old Oldsmobile station wagon as its teaching car. The car had hand controls installed. They were simply attached to the pedals of the car with a pulley system along the steering column. When the driver pushed down on a handle, it pushed down the brake pedal. When the driver pulled on the handle, it pushed down the accelerator. A spinner knob (also known as a suicide knob) allowed the driver to steer with one hand.

It was not hard to learn. Walking folks have trouble because they instinctively use their feet and then hands, too; consequently, they often stop and start abruptly. Without the option of foot control, the problem disappears. It is relatively easy to drive a car with hand controls; reaction times are much faster than with the foot.

One practical problem for me was I was still not able to fully compensate for my lack of torso muscles, so balance was an issue. There were a few circular curves that left me leaning to one side or another in the car, but I soon learned to compensate and learned where all the armrests and other balance points were. Eventually, I had to retake the driver's test to get a new license authorizing driving with hand controls. I also had to get special insurance, as I was seen as a driving threat because of my physical condition. The next big hurdle was learning to get me and my wheelchair into the car. I'll describe the process later.

Despite this new freedom, or maybe because of it, it took me a while to realize walking was not really on the agenda. But the implications of what it might mean hadn't yet taken shape. I was still very much caught up in what I could and couldn't do and what I could and couldn't feel. Things changed every day.

I spent more than seven months in the rehabilitation center. I shared the joys and pains of my fellow patients and grew to know them and their families. I learned about their hopes and dreams and shared their everyday frustration, courage, and determination. Not all had supportive families or somewhere decent to go upon leaving, circumstances I was fortunate to have. It was humbling, and I realized I had no reason for self-pity — even if I had an occasional lapse.

At one point during my long recovery, the facility's director promised never to kick me out before I was ready. When he made the promise, I had interpreted "ready" to mean up and walking. But now, six months later, walking was not even a remote possibility. Now I needed to find out when and what "ready" really implied.

Dr. Richard Sullivan, the director of the rehab center, was a kind, well-intentioned man, calm and solemn. He was handsome, with wavy hair streaked with gray, and always wore his white doctor's coat over a smart business suit. He agreed to meet with me privately in his office. I don't think too many actual patients had done this. These were the days before HIPPA (the Privacy Act), and mostly, it was parents or relatives seeking answers or solace who spoke with the director, not the patients themselves.

However, I was technically an adult, all twenty-one years of me, so I asked Dr. Sullivan what my outlook was, medically and physically. I could tell he was trying hard to be honest in the kindest way possible, which I appreciated. He told me to expect my current condition to be stable. It was what it was going to be.

His next words rang in my ears and haunted my heart. "Life can still be good," he said with a patronizing smile.

"Not good enough," I replied with a flash of anger.

A receptionist named Hazel worked in the rehab center. She had a disability requiring her to wear full leg braces and use crutches. She was in her fifties, with a head of curly gray hair. She was sweet, friendly, and willing to talk. She was single and seemed to enjoy her job. Each night, she hiked into the reception area through the front door of the center on her crutches for the evening shift. For her, hiking meant thrusting out both crutches ahead of her and then dragging her legs and the heavy braces forward to meet the crutches. Again and again. It looked exhausting.

She remained seated until leaving time when she gallantly hoisted herself onto her crutches and, with obvious extreme effort, "walked" out the nearby door to go home.

Hazel was held up as the success story of the rehab center. She was a fine example of what a person with a mobility impairment could achieve. She flashed through my mind when Dr. Sullivan said, "Life can still be good."

As lovely as she was, I was not going to be like Hazel.

In the early 1970s, people in wheelchairs stayed home. The medical profession concentrated on repairing physical damage. Once you were as fit as you were going to be, you were on your own, which usually meant the only place for you was with your loved ones. (Ask any severely injured Vietnam veterans what support mechanisms were in place. There were few.)

I had few practical skills, not much work experience, and no glowing talents. I was just a student, and the little work I had done was waitressing, which required walking. My family was solidly middle class. For us, there were no grants or tax allowances that my parents could access to assist in converting the family home into a place to accommodate me. There certainly was nothing to aid me in living independently.

I had to find a way to become educated and marketable. The only services provided by the government were low-income-based, so unless my parents kicked me out of their house, I would not qualify. Even if I did, it would require going to wherever they had an opening, probably in New Jersey. The only government-sponsored help we could find was a vocational rehab department. It was a state program for people with special needs to help them return to work, usually at basket weaving or sewing. This program agreed to pay my tuition but not room and board for my final year of school.

Dissatisfied with this option, I spoke with my friend, Tommy, a colleague at the rehabilitation center. Tommy was close to my age. He had been out on a boat one day and decided to dive into the water. Unfortunately, he dove into the wrong spot, smashed onto the bottom, and became quadriplegic. Tommy and I devised a plan, with our parents' help, to return to college. We enrolled in night classes at the nearby Seton Hall University. Our parents provided transportation.

Finally, I was strong enough to attempt an occasional visit to my parents' home. My parents and brothers had to carry me everywhere, which tarnished what should have been a rewarding experience. Eventually, we were able to install a lift to the back door of the home. My recollection was it cost about $900 back then, and it turned out to have a $35 lawnmower motor. But it was supposed to change my life, as I could now come and go independently.

Unfortunately, the lift was not reliable. We named it "Morris" after a finicky cat in a TV ad. "Is Morris working today?" was frequently heard. Because my bedroom and the bathroom were up a flight of stairs, I ended up sleeping on the pullout couch in the family room during most of my weekend visits. For showers, I gave Dad an early warning, and when he was ready, he carried me upstairs and sat me in a chair placed in the tub. My mom took over from there. My parents could not do enough for me but never coddled me, either. In our house, we lived by a rule "*Sympathy* is in the dictionary, somewhere between *shit* and *syphilis*."

Morris was the only adaptation to our family home, and it didn't add any real accessibility. Since I was expecting to return to college, we decided to work with the house as it was. We didn't have the finances to build a new wing, and as an adult, I had no intention of living at home with my parents.

Slowly, I eased myself back into the community, moving around in my new wheelchair and revisiting the familiar places where I used to run or cycle. It forced me to address my new reality. The few people I saw with mobility impairment, at best, worked behind a counter or held out the can at charity events. They were considered inspirations just because they had the courage to leave the house.

I was having nothing of this. I was determined to do far more than "still have a good life," but it meant I would have to design it on my own because there were no role models to follow or counselors to motivate.

Frustratingly, each time I made a positive decision on how to move forward, life contrived to knock me back. This time, it was the insurance company. My disgraceful experience with them gave me a taste of the indignation suffered by millions at the hands of uncaring, money-grabbing concerns and sowed the first seeds of my legal career.

I came home from rehab one weekend to find the insurance company representative visiting, along with a court reporter. They began questioning me and taking a legal deposition. By the wording and nature of the questions, it soon became clear to me they were trying to prove my girlfriend, Jane, not her parents, had owned the Camaro involved in the accident. If I could confirm Jane was the actual owner, it meant the car should have been insured in Jane's name and not as a named driver on her parents' policy. If they could prove the car was fraudulently covered by insurance, they wouldn't have to pay up. They were trying to bully me to, metaphorically speaking, throw my friend and myself under a bus.

Suspicious of their underhanded tactics, I was only interested in the truth and stubbornly refused to say anything else, much to their annoyance. My dad later said it was the day he knew I would become a lawyer.

The insurance company reluctantly conceded and paid for my hospital bills, a car converted for me to drive, and a small lump sum. My dad invested it, and the income paid for my university tuition and supplemented my income enough to cover the extra costs of learning to live differently.

As the final days in the rehab center loomed closer, I was forced to give some serious thought to what my future might look like. This closer look was prompted by a letter from my boyfriend. He had dumped me.

Even though I'd worked out the breakup was inevitable, it was still heartbreaking to see it in writing. He was the only man I had ever had strong feelings for.

He had wanted to visit me from West Point after the accident, but I refused to let him. I was vain and wanted to look better before we met again.

When we finally reconnected, I had it all set up. I propped myself up on the family room couch with my legs crossed, I had my mom take the wheelchair away, and I held a beer in my hand. When Jim walked in, his face lit up. Then, when I tried to move, the light went out. Subconsciously, it was then I knew it was over. But determination is my middle name, so I persevered to bring back the light. We went for a drive. Manhandling me in and out of the car only two months after my accident was neither easy nor elegant; Dad helped, but he miscalculated. When he tried to sit me in the passenger seat, he was on my left instead of my right. He ended up sitting down in the seat with me on his lap and then extricated himself from the car. It was hilarious and miserable at the same time. When my boyfriend and I were finally alone and driving, we were still feeling awkward. Finally, I made him promise to tell me straight if he couldn't handle the new me.

He kept his promise to take me to the Army-Navy football game, but it was a miserable experience. People in wheelchairs were parked alone along the sidelines of the field like oddities in a sideshow. I was truly depressed by the experience.

Even before the accident, our usual method of communication was by letter because of our remote locations. I'd assumed this tall, tough military man was gutsy enough to tell me his true feelings to my face. It might not have made our split more bearable, but at least I would have felt some respect. Instead, to put it in today's parlance, he ghosted me. I felt like an ugly, handicapped woman that no one could love.

He hadn't written for ages. Finally, after months of checking the mail each day and hoping, I received his long-awaited letter, which made the obvious official. It wasn't a particularly personal letter, more of a "time to move on" communique.

However, the experience helped clarify my understanding of my new status. Finding a sympathetic partner and building a loving relationship that could lead to marriage was unlikely.

He and I reconnected recently via Facebook and followed up with a wonderful, three-hour Zoom reunion. I know now if I had felt like an ugly, handicapped woman, it was my fault and no one else's. The realization of it hurt terribly since being loved romantically had always been a major part of my life's dream. It wasn't so much fear of not being married. I was terrified of never being genuinely loved.

It took me a while to accept that parting wasn't about me. But I needed even more time to realize that the accident hadn't affected just my life. It wasn't just my accident. About two years later, when I was back in life and doing well, a family friend approached my mom outside of church and asked how I was doing.

My mom broke down in a cascade of tears.

While I was recovering, my friends told me about a growing movement to have women treated equally. At first, I did not understand all the fuss. My parents had raised us kids to be the best we could be. They said, "If you want to be a truck driver, be a truck driver, but be the best truck driver you can be." They didn't tell me to be the best housewife, best receptionist, or best secretary.

It took me a while to realize not every woman enjoyed the freedom, respect, and acceptance I did. I could have been a truck driver if I had wanted to. At home, my brothers and I rotated all chores, including dishwashing. The exception was taking out the garbage for fear of dropping the heavy can and redecorating the driveway. My dad didn't allow me anywhere near the cumbersome lawnmower either, though I was dying to try it. He knew I would probably cut off my toes if I did. These exceptions were based more on my clumsiness than on my gender.

I understood that being female helped to open doors in the literal sense. However, a woman in a wheelchair with a half-finished sociology degree was going nowhere professionally except behind a candy counter or reception desk. I needed a plan.

During rehab, I studied courses in child psychology and the psychology of adjustment. I figured the latter of the two should be an easy ace, considering my circumstances. My fellow patient, Tommy, and I had signed up for two classes each at Seton Hall University. We arranged our classes for the same time, two evenings a week. I had the same professor for both classes.

When I was wheeled in for the first lesson, the classroom went silent, which didn't encourage much interaction with the other students, but I was unconcerned. I was able to complete the courses and add them to my college credits. Now, I needed only a few more courses to obtain my degree. I signed up for summer school at Hofstra University in Long Island, New York. I needed to catch up.

Hofstra was progressive and fully accessible to people with mobility issues. It was not unusual to see other students in wheelchairs or with other assistive devices, and it was a good place to begin my transition into the real world. There was comfort there. I learned to drive to class locations in Big Blue, my Mercury

Montego MX with a brilliant blue body and a white vinyl top, and to wheel around the campus in my chair. The campus spread across both sides of a busy roadway; a covered bridge crossed the road and connected the two sides of the campus. It was not a flat bridge but had a steep ramp up and then a steep ramp down, but it did make access possible. Students at Hofstra were quite used to seeing folks with disabilities around, and help was never far away.

In the summer, a professional football team did its summer practices at Hofstra. We frequently spotted huge, muscled football players in the cafeteria. One almost ran me down at the coffee station. He stopped suddenly when he finally noticed me. When he finally stopped moving and took a good look at me, he resembled a deer in the headlights. He stuttered as he offered to fetch me a coffee. I saw his life passing before him as he realized what life in a chair might mean to an athlete like him. A few minutes later, I practically mowed down Joe Namath; he had to twist quickly to miss my chair. When he was injured for the game the following weekend, my fellow students said it was because of our near hit.

Gradually, a new confidence was taking shape. I even met a pleasant guy in the library. But life crashed again when, by a fluke, I found out he was married. His excuse for flirting? He felt sorry for me and wanted to cheer me up. I was upset and angry at the same time. I did not want anyone's pity.

I completed a full schedule of courses and was only one semester short of college graduation by the time summer school ended. I contacted my previous college in Washington, D.C., Trinity College, now Trinity University. They were happy to accommodate me so I could finish my degree. I took a single room with a private bathroom in one of the dorms. The doors were wide enough for my wheelchair, and with some adjustments, I could make it work. The school gave me a key to the back door of the main building, which had a small ramp providing access to a seldom-used door and an entry with no steps. I could park Big Blue right beside the ramp.

Now, I was back in business. Each morning, I got up, dressed, skipped breakfast, and headed to my car. I hauled my wheelchair into my car and drove up the hill to the main building, which was only a few hundred yards away. I parked there, got the wheelchair out of the car, got into it, and then wheeled up a ramp to a side door. I was the only student with a key to the side door. I wheeled to enter the main building, up a short ramp, into the basement. From there, I could take the elevator to the classrooms. Any time I wanted to go to another building, to the library, to the dining hall, and so on — I had to go back to my car and drive there. The school was extremely helpful and hospitable, as were the students. But it was 1971, well before the Americans with Disabilities Act gave voice and visibility to persons with different abilities.

I finished my undergraduate degree in December and planned to attend the graduation ceremony the following June with the class of 1972. But what was I to do next? I wanted to stay in D.C. I loved the place, and it seemed the right distance from my family.

I'd always been interested in social work, but after my first-hand experiences, being on the receiving end both in the hospital and rehab, my outlook had changed. I realized the actual job of a social worker tended toward administrative tasks, referrals, and the like. I preferred doing hands-on work. I wanted to be in the mix, helping real people with actual problems.

I learned a lot during my recovery both from my emotional roller coaster of a journey and from observing others. I was confident I could help people transition from rehab to home, or from hospital to home, in a hopeful, happy way. I could help them emphasize the positive, maximize their potential, and how best to maintain their dignity as their life transformed.

I worried about being typecast, though. I learned that people often make snap, negative judgments about a person they see sitting in a wheelchair. Unfortunately, they tend to jump quickly to the assumption I was someone to be pitied. I was sensitive to this tone of condescension, particularly from professionals.

How could I convince anyone that a person in a wheelchair working in the hospital was a competent professional? It was difficult enough for any woman to be considered a professional, let alone a woman in a wheelchair. I persuaded myself I needed to be credentialed and gain experience somewhere other than a hospital or rehab center. I needed to demonstrate my expertise was not just homegrown and that it would prove useful outside a hospital setting.

Graduate school had not been in my former life plan, but now it needed to be. I applied to the George Washington University (GWU) Rehabilitation Counseling program.

I received an appointment for an interview. Ironically, the school's offices were not wheelchair friendly. I had to park several blocks away and wheel to the front of the building. This was in the days before curb cuts. At each corner, if the curb was not too high, I turned around and dropped my wheelchair back over the edge, leaning my upper body forward to avoid flipping over backward. After making sure the road was clear, I scooted over to the other side. If there were no nearby driveways or other access, I waited for a pedestrian and asked them to bump me up the curb. Before they could even answer, I told them it was easy and directed them how. I received masses of help and some great smiles when the job was successfully done.

The front entrance to Building C, where the counseling classes were held, had about eight steps. Wheelchair ramps did not often exist in 1971. I had to sit outside the building and wait for a kind-looking passerby who could be persuaded to drag me up the steps in my wheelchair. As a shy person who hated asking for help even before I was mobility-impaired, this was a new chapter.

I had to dig deep to find a confidence booster to help me overcome my inherent reticence to put myself forward. I remembered the old song "Whistle a Happy Tune." So, I summoned up my courage, put on a happy face, and said, "Hey, you, would you mind helping me up these steps?" Over the years, I have done this hundreds, thousands of times, and only one person ever said "no." He told me he had a bad back. But he stayed until he could find someone else to help, as he supervised. One time on those same steps, the guy who helped me up said, "Weren't you at the Arena Stage Theater last Saturday?"

"Yes, I was," I said.

"I helped you there, too."

This was to be the challenge for the entire two-year program. But once in class, there was always someone to help me back down, especially my classmate, Willie, who used to bop me down quickly and then give me a spin at the bottom. I loved it.

On the day of my interview for the rehabilitation counseling graduate program, my outgoing qualities and mobility-impaired life management skills were still a work in progress. When I arrived and checked in, the staff was quite surprised to see someone in a wheelchair. After a short wait, I was ushered into the room with the professors/interrogators. They all had a "deer in the headlights" look as I stopped before them.

It was clear from their body language they had no idea what to do with me. This was a tad ironic for professors running a program dealing with counseling the mobility impaired, I thought.

The four of them introduced themselves and took turns telling me about the academic program in gentle, kind tones as if my brain was paralyzed, too. They asked me broad questions about myself, such as where I was from. It was obvious they were going through the motions to be polite. However, they made it quite clear this was a rigorous, two-year program involving numerous internships, hard work, and travel. I suspected they concluded I was incapable of completing the course.

Finally, they smiled sweetly, and the senior professor said, "Do you have any questions?"

"No," I said. "However, I think there is one you haven't asked me."

They acted surprised, sat up straight, and then looked at each other with a lost expression on their faces. Finally, one said, "What question?"

"How might I reply if someone asked me, 'How can you help me when you are mobility-impaired yourself?'"

They inhaled slowly in unison. After a pause that seemed like forever, one professor said, "And your response?"

"Point to the certificates on my wall," I said smiling sweetly. "With my BA and recently obtained master's degree from GWU. And then I tell them in addition to being fully qualified, I have excellent insight and firsthand personal experience. However, if these are still not enough, try the counselor next door. He can walk."

I waited for a moment and grinned.

It took a moment, but the room lightened. Shoulders relaxed, and the people became conversant and animated, even started laughing and sharing terrible jokes. They then asked if I was able to afford the cost of the program or needed a scholarship. I was awarded a traineeship/grant for full tuition and monthly expenses. It covered my rent plus basic expenses.

My pre-accident plan had been to share an apartment with three other college friends. Cathy, Mary, and Paula were also enrolling in graduate programs in D.C. They had roomed together throughout their college years at Trinity. They were fun and smart, and I enjoyed being with them. We decided to room together in D.C. since women did not live alone in those days. Tracking down a handicapped-accessible apartment had been tough, but eventually, the three of them found a two-bed, two-bath unit, and everyone was relieved. They signed the lease. I was home in New Jersey at the time, and they had to act fast. Unfortunately, when I checked out the apartment, I realized the doorways were too narrow for my wheelchair, and I couldn't access the bathrooms. We were flummoxed.

They were deeply concerned about finding something right for the four of us before classes were to start. I did not want them to stress out because of me, so I told them not to worry. They should take the apartment; I would find another.

As mentioned, in the early 1970s, women did not live alone. I was the first in my circle, first by necessity, because I had no other option. Again, my parents and I discussed it. Again, they accepted my logic and supported my position.

Mom came to D.C. to join me on the apartment hunt. We found an appealing two-bedroom apartment with two baths. The master bath had a straight entrance within the closet. The doorway was still too narrow, but I was able to buy a contraption I could put on my chair. When I wound the lever, the chair folded up and became slim enough to slip through the door. However, my feet then hit the vanity. I had to muscle the chair around to the right, but I could get in. There was also a second bathroom, but it was tiny and useless for me.

I tried having a roommate for a brief time, but she met a guy and left, which turned out to work better. I ended up preferring to live on my own. No one had to tolerate watching me struggle. No one was staring at the weird girl. With nobody hovering over me or checking on me, I could relax and vent my feelings at will. My frustrations were my own. It was my private, safe world, a place for me with nobody watching. It still is.

Two years, fifty-four credits, several internships, and one publishable article, including empirical research later, I earned my master's degree. My article was titled, The Need for Sexual Information and Counseling Among Traumatically Spinal Cord-Injured Persons. My roommate at the time came up with the idea, and I grabbed at it wholeheartedly. I remembered my conversations with Hi, Doc, and knew I was not the only person with this injury who was asking those questions. I wanted to ease the road for others and learn more myself.

Before the internet and Google, research was clumsier and took a much longer time than it does today. I contacted various organizations that worked with spinal cord-injured persons and read the studies they had done. I then developed my questionnaire on the topic. The clients at the rehab center where I was doing my internship were delighted to be my subjects — they were eager for some answers, too. Ultimately, I was able to support my theory of the strong need for sharing more information on sexual information with spinal cord-injured persons.

I was proud but exhausted and desperate to rebuild my mental and emotional strength. I had also been job-hunting and had a position to begin in the fall. But first, I needed to rejuvenate. I found the solution on another trip to Sweden to visit my pen pal and best friend, Lisa.

In the hospital after my accident, I was unable to use my writing hand for a while, so I asked Dad to write to some of my friends for me, including Lisa. (Actually Ulla-Lisa, but we Americanized her name.)

Lisa and I had been corresponding since I was in eighth grade. During my senior year of high school, my parents had agreed I should invite her for a summer visit. Lisa arrived in the summer of 1967. When she walked out of JFK Airport, she was the sister I had always wanted. We spontaneously hugged each other, and she was instantly my best friend. Not only was she as beautiful on the outside as she was on the inside, but she was also taller than I was. I felt free from my nerdy, tall awkwardness.

We'd spent the summer of 1967 traipsing around New York City, sewing matching outfits, hanging with my friends, and driving around in my parents' VW bug with the radio blaring, *Windy*, and *Don't You Want Somebody to Love*.

But now I needed to let her know things were different. I asked Dad to do it.

Dad wrote great letters, and this one was to be one of them. He told Lisa about my accident, what was occurring, and the prognosis.

Now it was finally time for me to visit Lisa in Sweden; I wrote to her and asked what I should bring. When she suggested I pack sneakers for long walks, I realized she didn't quite grasp my situation. But it had to be faced. I flew to Sweden, and it was wonderful. Lisa picked me up at the airport, and we drove to her family's tiny *sommerhus*, summer cottage.

A huge wooden man, made from tree branches and about six or seven feet high, with a smiling face, greeted me at the end of the dirt driveway. The wooden man's arms were outstretched, and there was a hole in his hand for flowers to be held in his fist. He was there to welcome me with flowers from the garden. The tree man was named August, and he wore a big smile. He was accompanied by Lisa's parents, Eva and Olof, who clapped in delight at my arrival. They had hoisted the Swedish flag to honor the occasion.

Like most homes, Lisa's family's summer cottage was basic, with no facilities for the mobility-impaired. However, they had figured out ways for me to navigate. Entry was by pushing me up the hill to the back of the house, where wooden planks formed a makeshift ramp into the family room. I could reach into the half-bath for washing up and the toilet, but full showers required a trip into town to the family apartment. The cottage was idyllic, and I was truly touched by the love, thought, and pride they had expressed in their efforts to make me feel welcome and wanted.

Every morning, Lisa's dad brought fresh berries from the garden for our breakfast. They seemed delighted with my visit and loved to chat and celebrate being together. We toured the area, went shopping in Alingsas and Gothenburg, and boarded a boat for a trip around the city port.

Lisa, her boyfriend, and I drove to Stockholm to stay with her relatives. We bounced through the cobblestone streets of the old city, stopping frequently to replace my feet on the foot pedals of my chair after they bounced off. They carried me down a curvy steep set of stairs to a restaurant that had been a sixteenth-century wine cellar. We celebrated their National Crawfish Day when I learned how to eat crawfish properly and arrange the empty shells around my plate.

My Swedish friends never saw my wheelchair as a problem. They relished overcoming any challenges or obstacles I presented. Their caring attitude made me feel whole again, and I enjoyed the challenge of finding a way to make things work.

Four weeks later, I returned from Sweden and finished gradu-ate school. Now, it was time to apply for counseling jobs. One of my friends from the graduate program had recently gotten a job as a probation and parole officer and enjoyed it. She said there were additional openings and suggested I apply for one.

So, I applied to be a probation and parole officer in the Com-monwealth of Virginia.

On the day of my interview, I was fortunate enough to grab a parking space right in front of the building. In 1974, there were no parking spaces for mobility-impaired drivers, so finding some-place appropriate was frequently tricky. I needed a spot where I could open my driver's door to its full extent to get my wheelchair in and out of the car. It also needed to be a space where people parking next to me couldn't park too close and prevent me from being able to get back into the car. End spaces were particularly good for this. At this time, I had traded in Big Blue for Blue Dot, a

VW Dasher. It was a more manageable size for me than the huge Mercury, which had felt like a boat.

To this day, despite having done it thousands of times, parking, along with filling the gas tank (everything has gone self-serve), are still the logistical banes of my life. I must customize the procedure for each vehicle and each gas station. Today, wheelchairs have improved incredibly in design and function. I currently use a rigid-frame chair. It doesn't fold as the original chairs did. I must first remove each wheel and toss them into the back seat of the car. Then I remove the chair's seat cushion and put it on the car's back seat on the passenger side. Then I take the back of the chair and tip it backward toward me. With leverage, I can pull it onto my lap. From there, I can push it onto the floor behind the front passenger seat, stowing it in the well area between the front and back seats.

Now, imagine going to a gas station with no attendant.

First, I line up the car so there is enough room for the chair between the car and the gas pump while making sure the car isn't too far away for the gas hose to reach it. I throw the seat of the chair over my chest and lean back on the door sill. I replace each wheel and the seat cushion, and then I heave myself in. As I wheel to the gas pump, I hope there is no rim or curb at its base keeping me from accessing the pump with my credit card. I also hope the credit card slot is not too high. It's an exhausting struggle and a gamble.

In the 1970s, wheelchairs were bigger, less flexible, and weighed close to fifty pounds. To put the chair in the car, I first had to jump out of it and into the driver's seat. I use the term "jump" loosely. It was more of a toss and controlled fall. I had a robust handle fitted above the inside of the driver's door. I gripped it to pull myself up and then launched my butt into the driver's seat. Then I picked up my legs, one by one, and placed them inside. Next, I removed the wheelchair seat cushion and tossed it into the car. Finally, I flipped up the footrests, folded the chair, and then grabbed it by the foot pedals and rested them on the door rim. I then scooted my butt back toward the passenger side, pressed the driver's seatback forward and down, reached over and grabbed the chair by the foot pedals, and then dragged it behind the front seats.

On the day of the interview, I was lucky to park successfully, then headed into the building to check in with the receptionist. After a long wait, I was given directions to the interviewer's office. I headed down a narrow corridor and nearly ran down an older gentleman exiting a door. He just managed to stop short, held himself from falling over me, and barked: "Are you Broderick?"

"Yes," I said.

"Wait for me in the end office," he said. "I'll be right back."

He returned and interviewed me. As I sat in his office, I noticed the big picture window right behind him and could see my car in its lucky parking space. The interviewer's name was Tony. He was short, balding, and resembled my girlfriend's Italian dad. He kept his head looking down while he was standing, but when he later sat down, he made eye contact. He was the director of the regional office, a man with progressive ideas and a desire to move up to the central office in Richmond, Virginia. He saw me as his ticket to a promotion, a demonstration he was caring, progressive, and innovative, all of which, it turns out, he was. In any event, he made me his mission. He told me he was going to offer me the job, but first, I had to do two things.

First, I had to rewrite my resume in such a way each of my prior jobs appeared to have "died without me." He said everyone was doing it, and by being excessively modest and humble, I was removing myself from the game.

Second, I had to list the things I could physically do and had done, as well as those I could not do because of mobility impairment. I listed some challenges I had accomplished, including waterskiing, solo travel, aerobatics, riding escalators, and negotiating street curbs.

He hired me.

Years later, he told me he had seen me extracting my wheelchair from the car before the interview. He said he decided then that if I was the applicant, the job was mine.

DOUBLE STANDARDS

During my four years as a probation and parole officer, I gained some insights into humanity. The job required me to match the same standards as the other officers. I welcomed it and expected no favors.

Part of my job was to carry out pre-sentencing investigations and make recommendations to the court on whether a defendant should be given probation or serve time in jail. These reports involved visiting the defendants, interviewing them, and frequently their family members. Because many front entrances were not accessible, defendants often had to physically lift me into their homes. Surprisingly, they were always willing and usually insisted on feeding me their staple home-cooked specialty — inevitably spaghetti.

We included the defendant's version of the offense in their presentencing report. Because they generally had pled guilty, there was no Fifth Amendment issue, and it was fascinating to hear their description of events. Bearing in mind that I could have up to sixty live cases at any one time, in all the different explanations I heard, almost never did one admit they had considered being caught or found guilty.

Only one had considered the consequences of the crime or its effects on the victims. The woman had been in a difficult marriage and felt ignored by her husband. In desperation, she had shoplifted at a local store, hoping to get caught. She wanted her husband to have to deal with her — to hear her, to notice her. Unfortunately, her husband used her behavior as a rationale for divorce court, and she was left alone with a new criminal record.

To complete our investigations, we also had to check state, federal, and local records for past criminal history and do employment checks, school verifications, and such. This was long before computers, so we made telephone calls or visited their neighborhoods to obtain information about defendants.

This often meant a visit to the courts, whose parking lot featured a slight incline. As was typical, no parking spaces were reserved for the mobility-impaired. When I was forced to park at the bottom of the incline, it was a real chore for me to wheel up to the top. On the bright side, on the occasions when I was accompanied by my friend and coworker, Cindy, we had great fun returning to my car. She stood on the two bars protruding from the base of my chair, held onto the back handles, and flew downhill to my car with me. It made us laugh and gave me a moment of freedom. But for the most part, I was on my own navigating the incline.

Because no one presumed a woman in a wheelchair to be a probation officer, I was able to surprise defendants by appearing to be a customer at their workplaces, such as retail stores, where I could verify them doing their job without alerting their employers as to their legal situation. After the initial shock at seeing me had passed, the defendants relaxed. Some even expressed their approval by saying "pretty cool" accompanied by a beaming grin. The defendants could never predict when I might show up; it kept them on edge. Some couldn't understand how I had gotten there. One guy asked me if I could lie down or had to remain permanently in a seated position.

Occasionally, my disability allowed me to disarm my clients. It sometimes helped when people had no idea what to do or expect.

For example, one day a client showed up at my office for his monthly supervision visit wearing huge scuba-diving flippers on his feet. He looked ridiculous as he tried to walk and accommodate the flippers. When I asked him what was going on, he explained he had arrived at the building entrance barefoot. A guard told him he could not enter without shoes on his feet. He had driven to the appointment barefoot, and all he had in his car was his flippers, so after some hassling by the building manager, he put them on and walked upstairs.

He told me he was tired of rules and stupid regulations, he was tired of people in general, he was tired of his parents' yelling, and he had had enough. He was depressed, everyone was against him, and he couldn't win. He pointed to the window behind me and said he was going to jump out.

I realized he expected, in my condition, I might give him sympathy. But I didn't think sympathy was what was needed. I thought he needed some tough love. So, I told him he could, if he insisted, jump out the window, but I added if he did, he still couldn't win. He looked surprised and asked why not. I said his parents were still going to have to pay for the broken window, and they would still be mad at him. He stared at me for a moment and then broke into a peal of laughter. He knew I had called his bluff.

Afterward, he didn't try any more "poor me" tricks. He was respectful, and he always wore his shoes for subsequent visits.

As it was for most places, courthouse access was limited for me. I found a way to enter through the back door. A nearby elevator provided access to other floors, but it did not make the courthouse fully accessible. Three steps led up to the area where the judges' chambers were, and four steps led down to the jail, where we frequently had to go to interview defendants.

For my first pre-sentence report, I interviewed a defendant being detained at the Fairfax County Jail. Upon arriving at the jail, I checked in at the front security door. The sheriff's people were accommodating and carried me down the steps.

I was excited to visit my first defendant behind bars. He had been charged with distributing LSD. He was a big-time drug dealer, or so I presumed, as I waited eagerly and nervously for the sheriff's deputies to deliver him to the interview room.

When they arrived, I was surprised to see he was just a kid, no scarier than either of my brothers. His offense had been sharing a packet of drugs with a friend. He was more frightened and more nervous than I was, and it was obvious he had learned his lesson. I completed my investigation and report and then attended his court sentencing. After assessing the defendant, the judge suspended his jail sentence, instead imposing a period of probation.

Another defendant had been convicted of selling amphetamines. His behavior had been surprisingly simple and, in its way, resourceful. He had legally purchased several packages of an over-the-counter product containing amphetamines. He had removed the items from their packaging and put the tablets in clear plastic bags. He then sold them on the street as amphetamines — which is exactly what they were. In the Commonwealth of Virginia, this action provoked a ten-year prison sentence. After explaining his behavior to the judge, he was instead ordered to complete a residential drug program and then complete probation. He managed to struggle through ten months of the year-long program, but one day, it all became too much for him. He phoned me and said, "I can't do this anymore. I need to leave this program."

"You can't," I said. "If you don't complete it, I will have to inform the judge. You will be brought back to court and sentenced to ten years."

"But I've had enough. First, they cut my hair, changed my lifestyle, and drummed the law into my head. But for two weeks now, I've done nothing but clean stairwells with a toothbrush. It's teaching me nothing, and I refuse to do it anymore."

"If you leave, I will have to get a warrant and arrest you."

"Okay, get your warrant. I prefer to go to jail. Are you coming to get me? I will wait where you tell me."

I collected my warrant and picked him up about an hour later. When he asked me to stop for cigarettes, I did. Then I delivered him to jail.

Something about the guy impressed me. He was not a hardened criminal. At his subsequent court hearing, he impressed the judge, who released him on probation. After completing his sentence, he went straight and never darkened the probation office door again.

Jail visits became commonplace for me. I noticed most of the prisoners were bored with so few activities or programs to help them. After a while, it motivated me to do more for them. I'd hoped my efforts might encourage them with a degree of rehabilitation into responsible citizens. At one point, my colleague Cindy and I assembled a group of inmates for weekly counseling. Eventually, we agreed with the guards that the only benefit we served our group of miscreants was a plausible excuse for them to spend time outside of their cells. Usually, they weren't interested in the counseling; they just wanted a chance to get away from their cells for an hour.

However, the short-lived counseling sessions were a chance for them to talk and for us to listen. In one session, an inmate complained society begins lying to you as soon as you are born. He said people try to trick you. For example, he said they tell you there is a Santa Claus, but it is all a big lie. He said no one should tell their kid there is a Santa Claus. For us, two young women from the suburbs, this was an interesting position to hear, and we tried to understand the bitterness he carried with it.

After I had been on the job for a couple of years, I was assigned to do the pre-sentencing report of a major case. The defendant in the case had gone to trial and had been convicted of armed robbery, several murders, and a serious assault. The charges stemmed from his decision to rob a local Roy Rogers restaurant. When he entered the restaurant near closing time, five or six employees were still there. He forced them to show him the safe location and then herded them into a walk-in freezer at gunpoint. He did not stop there. In the freezer, he shot each of the employees, then locked the freezer and left them there to die. Miraculously, one brave soul survived. Although seriously injured, he was able to identify the defendant and testify at his trial.

As usual, I was required to obtain the defendant's version of events. The sheriff's deputies were protective and hovered nearby when I interviewed him in the local jail.

The defendant thought himself smarter than anyone else in the room. It was also clear he assumed charming the little lady in the wheelchair was no problem. He took his seat in the tiny interview room. As he tipped his chair, leaned back against the wall, and answered my questions, he was enjoying himself. He behaved as if the interview was a game show, and he knew all the answers. However, I sensed a controlled fury in him as he explained the reasons he was truly innocent and how he would "beat the rap" at some point. His physical size, manner, and unreleased tension intimidated me.

I saw straight through his act. I suspect he read it on my face as he left the interview room. (I never have been able to perfect a poker face.) As the sheriff's deputies led him back to his cell, he slammed his fist into the plaster wall, leaving a jagged hole.

Later, I interviewed his family in my office, this time with no deputies protecting me. His family intimidated me, too. They made threats against the county prosecutor who had charged the defendant and conducted the trial. They claimed the prosecutor would be in mortal danger if he appeared in their county. They shared the defendant's hatred and suppressed anger against society, and they acted more like victims than antagonists. They held no empathy for the families who had lost loved ones. They said the defendant had nothing to do with it, and law enforcement should be looking for the right killer.

I personally reported their threats to the local prosecutor. The prosecutor laughed when I told him, but his humor was unconvincing, and the smile didn't reach his eyes.

As part of the pre-sentence report, we provided the entire criminal history of each defendant. Collating all this information, at least on state and local crimes, required me to physically go through stacks of heavy, awkwardly large, handwritten ledgers kept in the clerks' office. The clerks, ten or more women, sat behind their typewriters in a secretarial pool at the front of the room. Clerking was an acceptable job for a female in 1974. One clerk was assigned to each judge. The women were friendly and helpful and knew everything happening in the courthouse. I came to rely on them, and we often shared stories about our jobs and colleagues.

Delores clerked for the judge to whom I was assigned, a gentleman named Burch Millsap. He had a Southern accent and a mostly bald head, long before the saying "bald is beautiful." I appreciated his quiet sense of humor. One time, I told him how horrified I was to find gray hair on my head. He declared to be happy finding any on his. Over time, Delores, the judge, and I became great friends. We enjoyed discussing our jobs and swapping gossip. Delores routinely informed me about the judge's mood and concerns before I saw him.

On the day of sentencing, having submitted our report earlier in the week, probation officers often met with their assigned judge before court to answer questions or address outstanding issues. To reach the judges' chambers, I accessed the courthouse via the parking lot hill and the back door. I rode the elevator to the clerks' office on the third floor and wheeled along a maze of corridors ending with three steps up. After I had been working in the job for a while, Eddie Young, the main administrator, learned to be on the lookout for me. A man of small stature and a big heart, he yanked me and my wheelchair up the steps. To this day, I'm surprised we both didn't end up in a tumbled heap at the bottom.

Judge Millsap was always willing to share his reasoning, concerns, sentencing inclinations, and conclusions with me before a court hearing. He asked questions to help him to be sure he understood the defendant. Occasionally, he inquired whether any further report information made a difference or instructed me to follow up on an issue. My experience with Judge Millsap was equivalent to taking a course: "An Introduction to the Art of Judging Criminal Cases."

Learning how judges think firsthand was amazing. It provided fascinating insight into the many considerations involved in each seemingly simple decision.

When a fifty-five-year-old man was accused of picking up extremely young girls and either paying them cash or buying them ice cream to entice them to touch him, the judge was naturally curious as to how crazy, deep, and devious the man's issues might be. It turned out the defendant was an uneducated man. He was small in physical size and mental capacity. To his mind, his behavior had not been a crime at all; he figured it was acceptable to ask for the girls' touches if he paid for it.

The judge believed if this man were sent to the penitentiary among more hardened criminals, he was likely to be killed or raped because of both his physical stature and the nature of the charges. Consequently, the judge crafted a unique sentence to address the issues, one allowing for jail time but avoiding the penitentiary.

Sometimes, Judge Millsap delayed sentencing to give defendants a chance to demonstrate improved behavior and be rewarded with probation. His decision frustrated me, and when I asked him about it, he told me some people need to keep making mistakes until they understand there is no one else to blame but themselves. Judge Millsap studied each case individually. He worried about who could "survive" in the penitentiary and who was at risk. In the latter cases, he tried to fashion a sentence to keep the defendant in the local jail instead of "The Big House."

Judge Millsap taught me about diversity and embracing people's differences while applying the law appropriately. I didn't even realize I was being mentored.

Writing the pre-sentencing report was the beginning of probation officers' duties. Once we had filed the report, we were required to appear in court on the sentencing day and explain and be ready to defend and support our recommendations. We could be called to the witness stand to be questioned and cross-examined (i.e., questioned) on our findings.

One case involved my cross-examination on the witness stand by one of the hotshot lawyers in town. The word was out, and the courtroom was full to observe the master "take down" the witness. But I wasn't a novice anymore. The lawyer asked some dumb questions, looking for a big score.

This one, for example: "Ms. Broderick, you claim in your report that the defendant obtained a new boat for only fifty dollars. Now, how, and where do you buy a new boat so cheaply?"

"The statement came from your client," I replied, "and I assumed he meant the boat was new to him."

"You knew I was representing him. Why didn't you call me?" asked the attorney.

"You were aware I was drafting this report. Why didn't you call me?" I replied.

I loved the banter. It was the day my love for the courtroom began to germinate. I was learning my craft, and I could now testify with confidence in my work and my ability to answer questions. I liked the challenge of being put on the spot and needing to find the right answer. I was proud of my work, and I enjoyed surprising people who did not expect such competence from someone in a wheelchair.

A different case ignited the flame of an idea: Perhaps I could become a lawyer. I had prepared a pre-sentencing report on an African American man who had been charged with an incident involving a gun. On questioning him, I could not understand why he pled guilty. I went over and over the facts with him and completed a full investigation into his background. He impressed me as a truthful and gentle person.

The incident happened while the defendant was working a second job as a security guard. He'd been standing outside the restaurant he was guarding when two intoxicated white men approached and began to hassle him. He attempted to diffuse the situation but refused them entry to the family-friendly restaurant in their condition. The men became enraged and physically attacked him, pinning him to a wall and pummeling him. Concerned he was going to be seriously injured or killed, the defendant pulled out his gun and fired a shot into the air as a warning. Nobody was injured.

In my pre-court meeting with Judge Millsap, he asked me why I thought the man had pled guilty to those facts. I found it difficult to explain, but he persisted. Finally, I plucked up the courage to say, "I suspected that as a Black man living in Virginia during 1976, he'd been advised it was best to accept the plea offer."

In the court hearing, the judge did something unusual. He offered the defendant an opportunity to withdraw his guilty plea and took a break so that the defendant could think it over. The defendant came to me and asked what he should do. I informed him I could not give him legal advice and that he needed to talk to his lawyer, but I usually did what a judge suggested.

The defendant withdrew his plea, was appointed a new lawyer, went to trial, and was found not guilty.

Sometime after, his original lawyer wrote a nasty letter to my bosses and Judge Millsap, hoping to get me fired for acting like a lawyer and giving legal advice. The letter never mentioned the defendant went to trial and was found not guilty, a verdict for which most defense lawyers were usually grateful.

I was devastated and went to discuss the letter with Judge Millsap.

"What should I do?" I said.

"Why don't you do what we judges do?"

"What?"

"Take a big gulp," he said.

This response was remarkably unsatisfying. I waited to hear the rest, but he'd finished. However, I couldn't leave it at that.

"I was shocked the defense attorney was not happy to find an innocent man not guilty," I said. "Even I could do a better job than he did."

The judge looked at me, waited for full eye contact, and then said, "Why don't you?"

Which is how my legal career began.

DIPLOMACY?

Not long after rejoining the academic and social worlds after rehab, the real effect of being a person who lives differently began to sink in. Although most people are kind and looking for ways to help me (whether I need it or not), they offer it with a sense of sympathy bordering on pity.

When people discover I am a professional with master's and law degrees, they usually overplay being impressed and inspired. But they are truly dumbfounded when they learn I live alone. "You are so brave," they say, or "How?"

Someone once asked, "How do you sweep?" (Answer: I put one hand on the broom and then the other...) But I do enjoy innocent questions from kids, especially the little girl who kept looking under my chair for the hole and asking how I go to the bathroom.

At conferences or social events, people often puzzle over why I've shown up. Nobody asks me what I do, just where my helper is. Eventually, I heard they didn't know what to say or how to act. I confront this attitude every day, and at times, it can hurt down to my core. Am I so unapproachable? I'm a girl in a chair not an alien.

In every new situation, I'm appraised and judged before even opening my mouth. It is remarkably easy to notice how people dismiss me as soon as they see me. Sometimes, you see a flash of panic when they don't know what to say or do. At other times, their eyes wander, or they suddenly put on an overly bright smile and take on the tones one uses when talking to a small child. They might even pat your head.

One day I was riding on an elevator with friends. When the doors opened at one of the floors a woman looked in at us and asked, "Is she going down?"

"Yes, she is," I responded. "And she talks."

Most of the time, I try to curb my tongue. In an ideal world, I shouldn't have to, but I do because my only other choice to remain sane is to lock myself away from society, out of sight and mind which I refuse to do so restraint is called for. I must keep my emotions and tongue in check to get on.

My challenges are greatest when I am traveling. Traveling "differently" has delivered marvelous experiences, understandings, and misunderstandings. I've absorbed a whole new perspective of the world, its cultures, and its diversity. Travel has rescued me from isolation, but on many occasions, it has tested my resolve.

INCONVENIENCE OR
ADVENTURE?

Every time I travel, and there have been many journeys both for work and pleasure, it is just a question of time before something happens to test my restraint. But, instead of saying what I was feeling, I have learned to treasure each journey as a heartfelt adventure, including its potentially annoying moments.

I recall a trip to Bangladesh. I flew to London, where I boarded a jet bound for Dacca. For about fourteen hours, the passengers were jammed three across in the airplane seats, squeezed in like sardines. The foot area was stuffed with suitcases and travel paraphernalia, so my knees were against my chest as my feet rested on the suitcase on the floor in front of me. The overhead bins were packed, as the flight was fully booked. There were families, children, toys, and food items everywhere in semi-controlled chaos. The plane was so crowded and uncomfortable that I wondered if we had surpassed the weight limits and could take off. After many hours in a cramped and jammed position, the flight seemed endless.

Eventually, we landed in Dacca. I had come to visit friends who were working there and to experience a new part of the world. As usual, because of my handicap, I was to be the last off the plane. This is typical for a person with a mobility issue, as the airlines do not want to make all the passengers wait for one person.

As the crowds slowly and loudly left the plane, the baggage, food, and paraphernalia disappeared. Finally, I was able to rest my feet on the floor. I was exhausted but tried to be patient. I was also excited and relieved to have arrived. The relief did not last long. The airplane was cleared, and I was the only passenger left aboard. Nothing happened. I waited. Nothing happened. I waited. Nothing happened.

The cleaning crew came on board but cleaned around me. Finally, I was approached by two gentlemen in airplane company uniforms. They spoke to each other while looking at me. Then one of the men spoke to me in English.

"Can you walk?" he said.

"No," I said.

"Well, how will you get off the plane?" he said.

"You must help me," I said.

The men left, deep in discussion.

I began to feel nervous I might be stranded on the jet. Fortunately, one of my hosts had foreseen this possibility and had made his way onto the aircraft. He spoke to the head flight attendant and explained the situation. They made a plan to carry me off the plane together. My friend later informed me that in their Muslim culture, men were forbidden from touching an unmarried woman in public. Consequently, no one wanted to lift me out of the plane.

As we headed into the terminal, uniformed men on bicycles with rifles casually hung from the handlebars greeted the newcomers. It didn't surprise me, but I was astonished when, after retrieving my luggage, a crowd followed me out of the airport, pushing and shoving to look at me. It turned out wheelchairs were rare sights there. At the taxi line, they stayed just to watch my attempt to enter the cab. As I maneuvered, an onlooker assumed I was falling, reached out, and grabbed me. There was a communal gasp, and then, a hush fell over the crowd. The kind gentleman left with his head bowed, ashamed of trying to help me; he'd broken a religious protocol.

Children found me unusual in Bangladesh. My friends took me to see the local streets. Kids swarmed around me and asked questions. They were happy, energetic, and loved to talk. My host spoke Bangladeshi, so we were able to communicate.

I asked one little girl how old she was, and she said she didn't know. My host explained it was typical. The girl explained she had been born the year after the flood, which was the calendar there.

As we walked back to our car, we heard a loud clattering. A long, flat wooden wagon with wooden wheels pulled by two trotting mules was approaching. A Bangladeshi man in worker garb, wearing a large, straw-brimmed hat, stood in the front of the wagon with his arms outstretched, holding the reins. It was a stirring sight, and I raised my camera to take a photo as he neared me. When the mule driver saw me, he threw his arms up in the air even higher in excitement, broke into a huge grin, and yelled a hearty greeting.

In Bangladesh, people were surprised to find I was not asking for money. There were beggars everywhere, and people lived on the street. I saw a young man on the sidewalk use a hose to bathe himself inside his wraparound tunic. He twirled around in the garment as if doing a scarf dance with water. He never exposed himself and was fast and graceful. It was said that the most successful beggars were those with visual impairments or blindness. According to the local lore, it was common for desperately poor parents to cause their children blindness to better support the family.

The friends I visited worked for the Helen Keller Foundation. They learned that many of the blind people were victims of a vitamin A deficiency. The foundation was trying to teach people to use vitamin A to prevent blindness.

We took a quick trip to Katmandu, Nepal, an exotic and colorful place with a spectacular bead market. Women were selling more beads and jewelry bobbles than I had ever seen in one place in my life. We also visited the ancient city and a few temples. Some featured pornographic engravings along the bottom edge of the roof. I was told the Goddess of Thunder was a virgin, and the engravings were intended to scare her and her thunder away. I confess I did not hear any thunder while there.

Although close geographically to Bangladesh, Nepal was a culturally different story. No one came near me, and no one offered any help. I learned that people looked at me with suspicion and steered clear because they believed disability was a punishment for an evil former life. When visiting the old part of Kathmandu one day, a crowd, initiated by curious children, began to follow me. The crowd grew as we strolled along until finally, there was shoving and pushing, and we were being forced down the road. It became sufficiently frightening, so we returned to our vehicle and moved on.

In some countries, I was treated simply as an item to be moved. Passing through Tokyo's airport, none of the people who came to help me disembark or re-embark spoke to me personally or acknowledged my requests. Even when it was clear they did not know how to transfer me from the plane to the airport lobby, nothing I said or did solicited a response. Eventually, I was placed into a truck-like vehicle and passed on to the next location, like a refrigerator in a crate.

On my first trip to Bangkok, it took about eight airport employees to take me off the plane. Again, it was 1982 and way before any ADA awareness. People in wheelchairs simply didn't travel, so there was no set procedure on how to offload them from the plane. It was haphazard. In this instance, they brought my wheelchair into the plane from the hold, and then they lifted me into it. After I was in the chair, they lifted my chair — with me in it — above their heads and proceeded to carry me (I was facing backward) down the stairway of the plane to the macadam and a waiting bus. It was terrifying. I tried to make suggestions but could not make myself heard, and none of the helpers understood English. I looked at their name tags to see if I could address someone personally, but I could not read the Thai lettering. I was totally in their hands. After their daunting effort had landed me successfully on terra firma, everyone simply ignored the wheelchair and me until they had to deal with it again. I became invisible to them.

Some of these experiences terrified me, but each time I survived, the relief sent a thrill buzzing through me, which made me braver and more willing to face the next obstacle. I was fascinated by these experiences and the challenges they presented. They became an integral element of the journey.

My parents had joined the International Senior Executive Corps and had been sent to Alexandria, Egypt, as part of the program. The program sponsored retired, skilled professionals as volunteers to teach their skills to willing partners in third-world countries. My retired flavor chemist dad was attempting to share his knowledge of flavor making with Egyptians interested in acquiring skills in the subject. I had the opportunity to join my parents there for a few weeks.

One day, my mom and I were walking down a hilly Alexandria Street to reach the market. Unfortunately, the cars were parked so close together there was not enough room for me to move off the curb in order to cross the street. My mom and I kept looking for a gap between the cars, to no avail. Suddenly, we heard a shout. We looked in the direction of the noise and saw a young man gathering friends and waving at us. They pointed at a car. They went over to the car, which had its window open, and opened the door via the window. Then, they all pushed the car out of the way so I could pass through. They then ran across the street to move the car so I could enter the block. They then replaced both cars, leaving me room to return. With huge smiles, they waved me on my way. The people were amazing. Several days later, when we were checking out of the hotel, I received my first offer of marriage — from one of the hotel employees.

I am awed by the kindness of people all around the world. I have never been left stranded, and I have witnessed the genuine smiles of joy and compassion of those who have rescued me. Traveling has helped me to learn the differences and similarities of diverse cultures. These experiences expanded my horizons, restored my faith in humanity, and taught me lessons I treasured when I was back home in my safe space, away from prying eyes.

When you live in a wheelchair, adventure is always around the corner. I love the challenge of finding a way to do things I am not supposed to do. Each trip brings unforeseen challenges. When the challenges at home get too great, the new challenges of a great trip are particularly rewarding and help to diminish the frustrations of everyday life. After an ambitious trip, coming home to my safe, accessible home sanctuary suddenly seems easier and sweeter, and everyday obstacles seem smaller.

I like the GK Chesterton quote, "An adventure is only inconvenience rightly considered, and inconvenience is only an adventure wrongly considered." This concept has guided me through my life and its many obstacles and has helped me see the beauty and fun to be found when things are viewed more positively. With this attitude, I began to see the wonders I was missing. Consequently, I have turned many potential obstacles into great adventures.

In 1974, I was returning from visiting friends in Crete and was transiting alone through Athens. When it was time to board the plane, there was no jetway. An open-air trolley carried the passengers out to the aircraft, which was parked quite a distance out on the tarmac. There were, of course, steps up to the trolley. Thankfully, a man had been assigned to transfer me to the plane and dragged me up the two steps onto the trolley. He was a huge hulk of a man with thick black hair and a craggy face. He did not speak English but acknowledged me with a friendly grunt or two as we trundled off.

When we arrived at the jumbo jet, I spotted it was accessible via a mobile outdoor stairway. Based on the spirited Greek words exchanged between my helper and crew, I gathered the man was to carry me up the flight of stairs at least two stories high. He and the flight attendant approached and confirmed my hunch. The hulk heaved me up with his big, strong arms. The flight attendant handed me my book, purse, duty-free liquor, and seat cushion, and we proceeded up the steps. At the top, my muscular helper was gasping for breath.

The flight attendant requested my seat number. I couldn't remember it, so she asked to see my ticket. I handed her the cushion, book, and liquor as I located my purse. Still reclined in the man's arms, I fumbled for the ticket and boarding pass. When I read the seat number, the flight attendant repeated it in Greek for my helper. It was something like fifty rows back. The loud sounds coming from my handler telegraphed that he was not pleased and wanted none of this or me. He started yelling and tried to gesture, despite me, my book, and my purse still in his arms.

Finally, sensing his distress and realizing desperate measures were called for, the flight attendant offered to help. She grabbed me under the knees to help redistribute my weight, thus allowing my handler the opportunity to readjust and grab me under the arms. Theoretically.

Well, he did readjust. But he did not take me under my arms.

He cupped each of my breasts in his massive hands and began to back down the aisle. I was a tad stunned and was about to open my mouth to protest. But then thought of two flights of stairs and fifty rows. Let him enjoy it, I thought as he placed me in my seat with great aplomb. With a wink and smile, he walked away a happy man.

While in the Greek Islands, I was camping with friends in their pop-up VW camper. I met the married couple while working together as probation officers. They decided to go on a great travel adventure and invited me to join them at one of their stops along the way. I met them in Crete. They slept in the pop-up section while I took the lower deck. When we got up, my bed transformed into a couch with a table in front of it. We were sitting there eating breakfast one morning when a Greek priest walked by. He was young and handsome with a full beard, a long black cassock, and a wide-brimmed black hat. He stopped for a chat. The husband had studied ancient Greek, was a seminarian in his earlier life, and was able to converse with the young priest. During the conversation, the priest continued to smile at me and occasionally gesticulated. When he'd gone, I learned he had inquired if I was interested in marrying. Ancient Greek could only go so far, so my friend was unable to explain my situation, but I found it charming and added it to my growing list of proposals.

We visited the Palace at Knossos, traveled to a southern beach to try nude sunbathing (where I learned we Irish get freckles everywhere.), and found a cool creek side spot to park the camper. A noisy racket woke us to find we had parked in the middle of the town's local fish market. It was thronging with activity all around us.

Later, we traveled through the valley of windmills, where we stopped in a small, two-road village to have coffee at a tiny outdoor establishment. The ground was unpaved, but the shop and a few tables were all made of stone. The village population was curious to see the out-of-town visitors. As we sat on the side of the road at our little table, I made sure the brakes on my wheelchair were secure since we were in a hilly spot. I was talking with my friends when I saw them smile and grin at something beside me. I followed their gaze and saw a little old man standing in front of my chair. He looked like he was about one hundred and ten years old. He had gray wavy hair and was stooped in stature. He was wearing the traditional black Cretan garb, black shorts, and a boxy black jacket. He blocked my wheel with a rock so my chair stayed firmly put. He smiled shyly and cast his eyes down as he backed away.

This was the kind of special moment that made the inconvenience worthwhile. To share a shy smile, see natural kindness and care, prompting an elderly man to protect me with a simple gesture and a rock truly touched my heart. I experienced similar gestures almost everywhere.

In 1988, I was traveling with two friends from Singapore to Bali. We had to transit through Jakarta, Indonesia. At Jakarta Airport, I was separated from my friends when it was time to board. Once again, I was wheeled to the basement area of the airport. There, two slightly built young Indonesian gentlemen were assigned to assist me. We went to the tarmac area, where they pushed me up to about five feet from a sedan and opened the rear door. I waited for a second and then said, "What now?" One of the gentlemen made a sweeping motion with his hand, indicating I should stand up, go over, and climb into the car. I looked at him and said: "I can't walk."

"What do you mean you can't walk?" he said.

"Don't you understand? I can't walk. I didn't bring this chair because I like the color. I can't walk."

The man's mouth fell open. He looked at his colleague and back at me and said, with a hint of panic, "Well, what do we do now?"

I instructed him to grab me under my knees and to have the other man take me under the arms and put me into the car. They followed the directions carefully and were pleased when they accomplished their objective without further problems.

They both got into the car and drove about five hundred feet; we could have wheeled it faster. I noticed the plane had a pull-down staircase at the back. The car stopped, and the two men climbed out and scurried around to the back to fetch me. They took my wheelchair out of the trunk and, with congratulatory smiles to each other, proudly settled me back in my chair. We turned around and faced the back of the plane. The two men had a brief discussion and then smiled knowingly again.

One picked me up under the knees and the other under the arms, as I had taught them, and we headed toward the rear of the plane. At the staircase, the gentleman holding my knees started up the steep steps first, tipping me backward so all the blood rushed to my head. As he neared the top, I thought I might pass out.

We finally reached the door, where I was leveled out once again, and my head cleared in a few seconds. The gentleman carrying my feet realized we had climbed the stairs in the wrong direction and decided to turn me around. Now, we proceeded down the center aisle of the packed aircraft headfirst. When we reached my assigned seat, I was facing in the wrong direction. There were some stifled chuckles as the entire plane watched the action. The two small men forgot I was not of Indonesian build or flexibility, and though they tried diligently, the laws of physics prevailed. There was no way they were going to get my five-foot-nine-inch body and themselves to complete a one-hundred-and-eighty-degree turn in a tiny airplane aisle. Of course, everyone watching had already figured it out, so it was quite a show. Finally, as realization dawned, they carried me to the back of the plane again, turned me around, and brought me to my seat one more time. When they finally put me down in my assigned seat, the entire plane applauded. I blushed, feeling as if I had unwittingly starred in a Charlie Chaplin-style comedy.

But the indignity was worth it for the opportunity to see Jogjakarta, its famous Borobudur, and then the island of Bali. In Jogjakarta, we were told a road led up the back of a famous Buddhist shrine, believed to date back to the eighth or ninth century. The shrine has a huge rectangular base supporting five concentric bases, topped with three circular platforms, and a *stupa* (dome-shaped shrine). I was able to reach the base and wheel around it, avoiding dozens of stone steps up the path on the front of the monument. My friends climbed to the top and took photos for me to see what it was like, while I enjoyed meeting other tourists at the bottom and seeing it from that perspective. Engaging with the other visitors and observing their attitude toward the religious monument was just as interesting to me as the monument itself.

From there, we continued to the extraordinary island of Bali. Although tourists come to enjoy the beaches, the Balinese believe there is evil in the sea, so they do not inhabit the beachside areas, only visiting to sell retail items there. Bali is a deeply spiritual place with thousands of temples, frequent parades, festivities, and customs honoring the gods, and an abundance of extravagant flowers, plants, and fauna.

We had arranged to rent a cabin in the town of Ubud. We had been told our cabin was wheelchair-accessible, and it was ... after two flights of stone steps. But accessible has many interpretations around the world. Back then in Bali, being accessible meant calling for help. At my summons, young Balinese men with huge smiles, wearing flowered shirts open to their ripped, muscular chests, carried my chair and me down to the grounds and up onto the porch deck. The place was a paradise, with bananas on the tree, coleus plants five feet high, and a young gardener who raked all the magnificent fallen flower petals from the grass each morning with a large branch broom.

As we moved around the island, I sometimes felt as if I was a tourist attraction. People walked up to me, smiled, posed, and suddenly, my picture was being taken. Even when I was passing parades of islanders in colorful clothes, carrying delicacies and tributes for the gods on their heads, or when I was approaching gorgeous temples, locals insisted on taking photos with me. And as always, they treated me to their beautiful smile.

We hired a driver to give us a little tour of the local tourist spots. He was a small, strong, middle-aged Indonesian man who spoke halting English and was intrigued by my wheelchair. He left briefly after a few moments and returned driving a van. He drove us around the island. He wanted to show us Mt. Agung, the volcanic peak presiding over the island, and a small coastal town where they dyed their roosters a hot pink color. He suggested we visit the Elephant Caves, but the downhill rock stairs to access them were not wheelchair friendly. I encouraged my friends to go on without me and report back.

While my friends explored the caves, the driver took me on a scenic ride. He showed me his favorite ocean view. We saw a workshop of women with sewing machines under a thatched-roof shed and passed a bare-breasted woman washing her hair in a stream. Extravagant flowers bloomed, and bubbling creeks sparkled everywhere.

During the drive, the driver bombarded me with questions about my disability and how I managed things. He was stunned to learn I lived independently and even more shocked I had a professional job. He told me he had a mobility-impaired son who couldn't walk. His son had not attended school and made a living by weaving baskets outside the shop run by his mother, the driver's wife. He asked if I was interested in meeting his wife. I was happy to agree.

We drove up to a parking lot, where the driver helped me out of the van and into my chair. He then walked away, returned a few minutes later with his wife, and proceeded to show her my wheelchair. He spoke in his native dialect in intense and excited tones. He gestured and pointed at me and my chair, explaining how the chair worked and how I was able to get around and be independent. His wife looked quite stunned as she took it all in.

The driver smiled broadly and continued smiling all day. Later, when he dropped us off at our cabin, he gave me a special little bow before returning to his van. I realized a new light had appeared in his tunnel of life. The thought warmed my heart, and I was grateful to be of service. I have always planned to live life with the expectations and actions of a non-disabled person, hoping others would realize I am just like them and there is no reason to fear the differences between us. I wanted to spread this message. Perhaps I did that day in Bali.

A NEW DIRECTION

I was wheeling through the Fairfax County courthouse and headed toward the rear parking lot. It was after an interview with another probation candidate. I'd decided to follow Judge Millsap's advice and apply to law school. I was feeling good about my future as I trundled along, looking around and absorbing the ambiance. It dawned on me how much I enjoyed working at the courthouse.

There was something magical about the place — a distinct feeling of reverence, a sensation like being in a beautiful church. As I stopped briefly to breathe it all in, I felt happy, joyful, and contented. And then I had an epiphany. It wasn't a conscious decision — more of a revelation, an understanding: *I wanted to be a judge.*

Because I had not yet even been accepted to law school, I had to push my Road to Damascus moment to the side. First, I had a long journey to travel.

Although I applied to several law schools, my first choice was the Catholic University in Washington, D.C. My decision was based on several reasons. The school had a ramp, and I'd had enough of battling with steps and prevailing on others to help me manage them. I had no desire to attend a so-called Ivy League establishment because I didn't care about prestige or the extra costs for what was arguably the same education. Catholic also had a good reputation for not being a paper-chase type of school, which better suited my learning preferences. It also had a good record of guiding its graduates into employment.

I phoned Father O'Brien at the law school every couple of weeks after submitting my application. I'd been informed he was a dependable contact, which proved to be true. Each week, he reported how my application was proceeding. He usually said, "Call back in a week." Each time, I did as instructed. One day, Father O'Brien called me and confirmed my acceptance. I learned later my perseverance had inspired him to persuade his colleagues, who had been skeptical about my physical capabilities and stamina, to admit me.

I began law school at the age of twenty-eight. As someone who had been out in the world and accustomed to a paycheck, I was not relishing a return to the relative poverty of my student days. I withdrew the retirement money from my probation job, which covered all my tuition fees. I redirected some of my savings — I was always saving up for my next trip — and my parents supplemented them when necessary.

After I'd worked out how to access the facilities at Catholic, I settled into my learning routine. It was February 1980. I may have been impoverished, but I was happy to begin the first phase of my dream career path and build toward a secure future under my own steam. During the early weeks of my first semester, I had to keep pinching myself. Here I was, studying law at a worthy university in the nation's capital. All I had to do was work hard, pass the dreaded exams and the even more daunting bar exam, and then I could look forward to a meaningful, well-paid job I enjoyed. *Not too shabby*, I thought, *for a wheelchair-restricted girl from the suburbs.* As the intricacies of law revealed themselves, I began to relish my studies with a new degree of clarity and understanding.

Even my social life showed a hint of promise. There was somebody special in my life. He was a fellow law student who never treated me as anything but his equal. We were comfortable together. For the first time since my accident, in the spirit of nothing ventured, nothing gained, I allowed myself to consider embarking on a real relationship. I was willing to try romance again, even though I had written off the possibility years ago.

I had arranged a special date to start this new journey, even though I was worried a strong come-on might scare him off. In any event, I was looking forward to our evening together.

But on that night, his behavior was distant.

"What's wrong?" I asked.

"It's not going to work out," he said.

I felt wounded. I had decided ours could be a wonderful relationship. All the right signs were there, and I was confident they were being reciprocated. But now, this.

"What do you mean?" I asked, struggling to stay in control.

He wept, which embarrassed him. He had told me he rarely cried. He tried to explain our relationship had to end, saying, "It just isn't going to work."

But it was all bullshit to me. It didn't feel like there was any reason at all. In the game of love, his rejection was just one more point for my disability.

I was first brave, then understanding, and then bitter. I tried to behave maturely about being dumped again, but I became slightly hysterical and depressed. Melancholy is one of life's greatest self-indulgences.

I called my friend and skilled counselor, Lois, whom I had met when I attended one of her workshops on how to interview sexual offenders. She was positively electric to look at, with her jet-black hair and huge eyes. She wore her kindness and compassion like a bubble wrapped around her, easily and obviously. At times in my career, when things had gotten difficult for me, and I needed guidance, I had called on her for some private help. She had changed my way of thinking and opened a new world for me, one bigger than just me or my issues.

Now, I needed to stop my sadness, but I had no idea how. I suspected Lois might have some ideas. I confess I was looking for a little sympathy, too.

"He broke up with me for no reason at all. Why, how could he?" I said.

"Call my friend, Etel," Lois replied. "She is a holistic healer and may be able to help you walk."

I sat there and thought, *Wait a minute. Lois is usually empathetic to what I'm saying. Why doesn't she hear me now?*

"Lois," I said, "don't you understand? He broke up with me."

"Call Etel," said Lois. But I didn't want to. Walking wasn't my immediate goal; I wanted to be loved. I had to sit back for a minute to listen to the voices reverberating around my cluttered emotional mind. I was puzzled about whether the voices were real or fantasy. I had worked so hard to believe life can be wonderful, albeit unconventional, in a chair. Now, I wasn't sure I could deal with the possibility of walking again. I knew the attempt could sap everything out of me.

I'd lived with this philosophy for ten years, and even though I was in a heartbroken state, I couldn't see any reason to change it. Still, Lois's words planted the possibility, and it nagged at me constantly. *Should I pursue this ... or not?*

As my mind batted the options back and forth, I felt stuck in a zone of never-ending twilight. The potential of walking hovered before me. Just thinking of it kept me awake at night. But then reality set in, and all hope was immediately smashed down by my ten years in a chair. *What if I allowed myself to believe it might, and then it doesn't work? Will I look stupid?*

After a restless, weepy night of confusion, I began to think more clearly. My initial reaction to Lois's words had been overshadowed by my would-be lover's departure. I'd bared my soul to Lois in the past. She had become finely tuned to my emotions and could identify my pain, even though I often had no idea where it came from. I knew she had my best interests at heart and was unlikely to steer me wrong. I conceded I should at least talk to her friend. And hey, if I ended up looking stupid, it wouldn't be the first time.

I phoned Etel DeLoach. She confirmed Lois had spoken of me and said she was keen to meet me. She told me she meditates with people all over the world at ten p.m. each night. She referred to this as "the healing hour" and invited me to find a quiet place on my own and join them in spirit.

I thought it weird, but she had piqued my curiosity. Curiosity was certainly more fun than a broken heart. I tried it one night. As instructed, I settled myself and meditated at ten p.m. After half an hour, I did not sense Etel or her community around me. Nothing at all happened.

But it didn't dampen my curiosity. Perhaps Etel could help me, even if she only helped me learn more about my body and condition. I wanted to meet her and discover what she was about. If I could benefit from her treatment, then fine. If not, it was also fine. However, I was conscious the desire to please Lois might have influenced my decision to try working with Etel.

My first appointment was scheduled for an upcoming Friday. The first obstacle was to get my body onto the table Etel used for healing. Leaping up onto tables was hardly at the top of my list of capabilities, and it was asking far too much for Etel to lift me. I needed to bring a physically strong person along with me to my appointment. But where could I find one?

Etel and Lois assured me a solution would appear. I admired their positive thinking, but I wasn't so sure.

Having committed myself to something I remained unconvinced about, I inquired about Etel. I half-expected to be mocked for even considering treatment from her. However, she appeared genuine and credentialed; she taught holistic medicine at John Hopkins University. I had no idea what this branch of medicine involved or how Etel practiced.

Etel assured me if finding a way forward proved too difficult, she limited my treatment to a maximum of three sessions saying she had no desire to string me along, raise my hopes, or replace my doctor. She hinted after our first meeting she would know more about how I might or might not benefit from her treatment. With this in mind, I redoubled my efforts to find a strong person to accompany me.

Less than a week before my appointment, I received a phone call from one of my long-lost cousins, who was to arrive in D.C. on Thursday and stay until Saturday. He was more than happy to accompany me.

Etel was a white-haired, elderly-looking woman, tall, round-shouldered, and with a kindly and no-nonsense manner. She worked privately out of her grand ranch house on a huge lot on a quiet road. As we drove into the driveway, Etel came out to meet us and showed us into her living room, where a portable massage table was set up and ready. My cousin heaved me up. I turned over onto my stomach, and Etel proceeded to work on me for twenty to thirty minutes. Because I had no sensation from the chest down, I didn't know what she was up to. At times, I felt pressure or weight in certain parts, and I could hear most of what was going on. At times, she did a little acupressure, but frequently, she was hovering her hands above my body. Sometimes I heard a crackling sound just below where her hands were hovering.

I heard when my clothes were being ruffled, and my body told me if it was being moved. I suspected she was working on my hip because I sensed my torso was lifted up and down from the table. But other than a few sensations and intuitions, I hadn't a clue what she was doing. And she was working so intensely, I was afraid to ask.

From his restless body language, I could tell my cousin thought the treatment was crazy, and he went to wait outside. Occasionally, I wished I could do the same. *Was this person a charlatan? Should I have faith in her?*

I stuck with the course. I had nothing to lose and, maybe, something to gain.

When Etel finished her treatment, she had me sit up and we talked for a while about what she required if we worked together. I was to eat no meat except poultry. Seafood was allowed plus lots of fruits and vegetables, organic and natural (big gulp from the daughter of the guy who makes artificial flavors for a living.)

I was still afraid of being disappointed should it all go wrong. My ego chimed in again. I was concerned about being called a fool for believing in an oddball form of healing. I also had a decade's worth of telling myself that a fruitful life in a chair was equally meaningful as a walking one. I was reluctant to cast this acquired philosophy aside and replace it with, "I'll do anything to walk."

As I wrestled mentally, new questions and doubts arose. Was I in a wheelchair when I didn't need to be? What if Etel was fixing something that could have been repaired a long time ago? What if I had been able to heal myself and hadn't done so?

I went home confused and fell asleep in front of the TV. I awoke later and noticed it instantly: My legs were going crazy. After ten years of nothing, I could feel them tingling.

My condition continued to improve over the next eighteen months as I worked with Etel. I successfully weaned off all medications, including Valium three times a day to control muscle spasms, with no side effects. I gained torso strength and balance, and eventually, I was able to do intermittent catheterization instead of indwelling catheterization. Without being over techni-cal, I didn't need a catheter in me permanently which meant I didn't have to flush it out with sterile syringes each morning nor have a bag filling with urine always strapped to my leg. Instead, at regular intervals, I inserted the catheter, emptied my bladder, and was done with no fuss. I still might not walk, but I did improve. My horizons were expanding.

I met with Etel intermittently, every six weeks or so, for her treatment, called the "therapeutic touch." I can't offer any medi-cal reasoning, but in the long haul, my balance improved as some atrophied muscles in my midsection went back to work. I was able to throw away my midriff brace, I was healthier and stronger, and my legs looked less like sticks and more like typical legs.

I am grateful to Lois, a person I trusted, for steering me to Etel. Her "psychic acupuncture" treatments didn't turn out to be just a fad I had read about in a magazine or watched on late-night TV. I could never have lived with myself if I had ignored this oppor-tunity. I'd have spent my life wondering what might have been. I would have been a coward if I hadn't at least given it a go. I had no choice; I had to try to walk. There was no failure in the effort. The only failure was not trying.

After about two years of treatment, it became harder for me to find someone who could lift me onto her table. Etel also grew impatient with me, as she had expected me to heal faster. Eventu-ally, we lost touch, and I heard she had left the area.

Later, I tried other healing approaches, such as acupuncture and acupressure, although I approached these treatments differ-ently and was not making walking my life's mission.

My attitude changed a lot with "the Etel experience." I realized there were mysteries in this world I could never understand and shouldn't close my mind to them. I wasn't walking after my treat-ments from Etel, but my health was markedly improved, and my life was more manageable. I was appreciative, grateful, proud that

I had tried, and glad movement had become easier. I could now live happily in my body. The bottom line had changed.

It was okay if I didn't walk, so long as the reason wasn't I hadn't tried. I was proud of myself for attempting the unknown and being willing to take chances. This mindset helped me to remain open to new options should any appear.

I was introduced to a man named Mike who did acupressure, could demonstrate impressive results, and thought he could help me. I worked with him periodically for a few years, eventually attempting to walk with braces and a walker. It turned out to be an exercise in fear, though. Wearing braces, I could stand. Viewing the world again from my full height of five feet nine inches was scary. Additionally, because my injury is at chest level, due to my poor balance, I can easily jackknife at the waist and fall forward. To counter this, I leaned all my upper weight on my arms to hold me up — but at the same time, I needed my arms to be relaxed to move the walker.

I kept trying. Some days, fear alone prevented me from moving even an inch. I made bargains with myself, such as *you can quit if you make it as far as the window.* It was incredibly exhausting and not as exhilarating as I had imagined. I felt like the process was taking over my life, and I was losing the sense of fun. Yet I had to try. But for how long and how hard? It was a solo journey. No one could answer these questions for me, and I would have to live with the consequences of my decisions.

I tried something new with Dr. Plekovich at the Miami Project for Rehabilitation, where I was given a battery-like machine. Electrodes, resembling sticky Band-Aids, were placed strategically on my legs, connecting me to the machine. I could turn the power on and off via buttons on a walker. Each morning, I spent about thirty minutes exercising. I attached the electrodes, turned on the power, and kicked my legs draped off the end of the bed. Over time, I could see my legs gaining muscle mass, and eventually, was able to kick with leg weights. Dare I return to wearing street-length dresses and skirts?

On a few occasions, I went to Miami, Florida, where I worked with the doctor and some physical therapists for about a week. Again, I trained in leg braces and electrodes and attempted to walk. This was exhausting, strenuous, time-consuming, and expensive. I had to travel to Miami and rent a hotel room and car because public transportation was not handicap-accessible at this time.

The results were marginal and energy-sapping. After a couple of years of treatment, I realized that in their current state, the electrodes and braces were only enough technology for some serious exercise. They drained the strength out of me and stalled my progress through life. It had been a lonely experience. Most of my friends thought my efforts were nuts and couldn't understand the process or its effects on me.

I decided I didn't want to focus my life on trying to walk again. I had places to go and things to do. There were other ways to attain fulfillment. I continued to keep my body in shape physically and was open to new therapies to explore. But mentally, I moved on.

Law school remained demanding, and I worked hard to get through it. During the winter months, I competed for and earned a place on the school's National Trial Team. The team prepared a mock trial and then competed with teams from other law schools who had prepared the same case. Several rounds led to the finals. To say budding law students were aggressively competitive was an understatement. For the regional team competition, we were to work in sets of two, as assigned by the coach.

I was disappointed because I wasn't paired with the person I thought I could perform best with. I was even more upset to learn the coach thought my designated partner possessed substantive knowledge of the law, whereas I was believed to be a good advocate. We were supposed to complement each other. My partner dressed the part and waved a large Mont Blanc fountain pen — not an item in the budget of a typical law student — as he spoke. He was tall, broad, and good-looking, but his self-confidence did not leak over to me.

It dawned on me that what the coach was implying with this pairing was I could speak well but didn't know much. Or he believed the little lady in the wheelchair needed a strong helper. It took me ages to come to grips with this, but it was one of the best lessons I learned in law school. The old saying was true: Ginger Rogers did everything Fred Astaire did, but she did it backward and in high heels. I could do everything my teammate did, but I was going to have to work harder and do it better.

My teammate, extremely sure of himself, took over the trial. I felt marginalized as a woman in a wheelchair — as if I were someone easy to push around in every way. He interrupted me and spoke over me when I was doing my part at the competition, and it seemed obvious he, at least, was impressed with his performance. He and I did not project a unified effort, and we did not fare well.

To his credit, my teammate later apologized. However, I could not put all the blame on him. I needed to learn to speak up. I needed to be seen and heard—not just in court but in life.

CHAPTER

13

BEGINNING AGAIN

By taking summer classes and working internships for credit, I'd finished law school in two and a half years instead of the usual three. This made me eligible to take the February bar exam. The bar exam, which you need to pass to be licensed as a practicing attorney, is given only twice a year in D.C. By taking the exam in February, rather than with all the new graduates in July, I had a head start on job-hunting, but still planned to attend the graduation ceremony at the law school.

I never expected to be so thrilled about graduation. It was to be a simple ceremony on a sunny day in May. I was excited because I hadn't fully taken part in my graduation from Trinity College, where, due to the accident, I was six months behind the remainder of the class. This time, I wanted to attend and enjoy the ceremony. I wanted the day to be special. All my siblings, their wives, children, and even a niece planned to attend, and we had arranged a special evening at my apartment afterward to celebrate the occasion.

The day was warm, with a cool, strong wind. The graduation hats didn't fit properly, and we were in danger of losing them in the breeze. We scurried around, trying to find bobby pins to hold them to our hair.

The graduates lined up in two rows, in alphabetical order, and then all hundred and fifty or so marched from the school to the huge Shrine of the Immaculate Conception (which the students fondly described as a pregnant elephant or a Russian Easter egg). Our seats were lined up along the side of the cathedral, on the hill. The professors, festooned in their academic garb, were stationed on a flat platform about halfway up the hill beside the speaker's podium.

It was only a few hundred feet from the law school to the side of the cathedral and our designated seating area. We were excited as we marched along, waving at friends and family, occasionally stopping for hugs. It was organized chaos of the best kind. We progressed up a side aisle jammed with family and onlookers. I was full of joy to be in the group, marching, instead of being in some special (separate but equal) location, and I felt a buzz of excitement.

As we approached our seats, an elderly woman jumped so suddenly out of the crowd in front of me that I nearly crashed into her. She grabbed my arm, put her face close to mine, and said, "Oh, dearie, I'm so proud of you. Isn't it just marvelous you could do this?"

I used to have an imaginary Kick List. It included names of the people deserving a good kick, should I ever recover such ability. This woman had just been promoted to the number one spot. Her words irritated me to the core. I wanted to tell her, "Look, lady, everybody sits when they study." But of course, I didn't. I had to be nice. Although I am sure she meant well, she had reduced me to feeling like a pitiable, handicapped person — just when I had been feeling as if I belonged.

The school had arranged for one of my fellow graduates to push me up a hill on the lawn to the platform to collect my diploma. It worked nicely, and I received my diploma like everyone else. Unfortunately, we had not completely thought the routine through. Everyone else continued walking across the platform and down the steps on the other side. But I had to turn around and pass the dean again as he prepared to give out the next diploma. There was a great deal of laughter and some extra applause on my second appearance, but my family was the group most responsible for such a raucous reaction. It helped me laugh and feel more real as everyone else laughed, too. This was not the "Oh, aren't you an inspiration, so brave" reaction a mobility-impaired person receives when performing a normal task. This was sincere and spontaneous, and everyone enjoyed a good laugh.

People in wheelchairs are expected to show gratitude. Even after fifty years of rolling around the world and experiencing outstanding kindness wherever I go, I prefer not to be the subject of a lot of fuss. But I understand it's a human trait to praise achievement in physically compromised people. The thing is that appearances are deceiving; having a physical limitation does not necessarily make a person inferior or unable. Sometimes, it heightens other senses in ways most non-disabled people never utilize.

For example, when I was first injured and could not turn my head easily, I found I could make my eyes look almost around the corner. My sense of smell heightened, and I could identify approaching people by the sound of their gait. These are not extraordinary abilities, but in most able-bodied people, they are underutilized. I have found ways to compensate for my lost skills; I have enjoyed the learning and the challenge.

The special evening more than made up for my daytime melancholy. I purchased a special dress for the occasion. For the first time since my accident, my legs were visible. Friends and family came around to join the celebrations. People brought me gifts, which made me feel guilty, and demanded to inspect the diploma, which I put on display in the narrow hallway. The food was great, and Dad played the perfect bartender.

To this day, people still assume achievement in a person with a mobility impairment is a rare thing. Disability is perceived as a weakness and a lack of competence. In 2021, an article entitled "Falling Short on Disability and Inclusion," published in *Washington Lawyer* magazine, noted most professional lawyers with a disability do not want to discuss their impairment or report it in surveys. The article quoted a lawyer with an impairment who said, "As disabled people, we work doubly hard to succeed so nobody can come back to us and say we weren't effective. We knew if we didn't do well, the next person [with a disability] coming along probably won't get a shot."

This has been my experience for the last fifty years. I have become best friends with the quirks of change. If it comes at all, it comes excruciatingly slowly.

Waiting for my bar exam results was more exhausting than a marathon. I was an emotional yo-yo, wondering if I had passed or not. Thankfully, a serendipitous distraction presented itself: I was summoned for jury duty.

I had often thirsted to be a trial lawyer with lots of courtroom work, so I knew it was an invaluable experience to be on the other side of the courtroom and learn what constituted a good lawyer presentation. I realized my chances of serving on a jury were slim, as most lawyers did not care for other lawyers, who explained things to the jurors, to be on a jury. Certainly, anyone with a car accident injury case would avoid me, too. But I could learn from listening, observing, and being with other jurors. I was assigned two weeks of jury duty and spent a large part of it in the jury room waiting to be called.

People were scattered randomly around the large room. Several Whist card games were underway, and the air was full of chatter. It didn't take long to realize jury duty was intensely boring. In one case I served on, though, I learned about jury dynamics, which served me well. When the jurors found out I had gone to law school, they insisted I was the foreperson. What a thankless task. The deliberations became a racial fairness game. If I let a white person speak first, someone pointed out that a person of color had raised their hand first.

We bring everything we are into the jury room. In my jury's case, we had to ask for reinstruction, and after, we stuck to the law and applied it as instructed. Nevertheless, we battled who we were and our own life experiences in reaching our decision.

Jury duty allowed me to be in the courthouse on the day the bar results were posted. This was before the age of the computer and anonymous tests. In 1982, if you passed the bar exam, your name was posted on a list hanging on the wall of the courthouse for everyone to see — but only if you passed.

It was about five o'clock in the afternoon. I was preparing to leave the jurors' lounge when someone I had taken the bar exam with, who happened to be clerking at the courthouse, saw me in the courtroom hallway. He was running at full speed but managed to yell over to me, "The bar exam results have just been posted on the sixth floor by the Court of Appeals. It's chaos up there."

Anyone who thinks a person in a wheelchair moves slowly did not see me that day. I spun around and headed for the elevator at warp speed, not even bothering to say goodbye to my fellow jurors.

No other university course I ever took compared with the stress of taking the bar exam. All the hours of study, the strain of the two-day exam, the costs of education, and years without a salary would be wasted unless I passed the exam. Unless I passed, I could not get a license to practice law.

While I waited for the elevator, I said to myself. "Patti, think positively. Whatever happens, you will not faint. You're going to stay coolheaded and alert and absorb the list slowly so you don't race past your name."

I pressed the button for the sixth floor, the doors clanged shut, and the elevator jerked upwards. The doors slid open to a scene of chaos. I rolled over to the wall, crowded with hopeful lawyers, and squeezed through the throng. They reluctantly parted to let me through. I parked in front of the list and read slowly down the names. Despite my efforts to remain calm, I held my breath.

My name was there. No mistake.

I exhaled. I smiled from ear to ear, and the knot in my neck instantly untied itself. I took a big gulp of air and felt the sting of tears in my eyes. I headed for the pay telephone. I had to tell someone. Mom answered.

"I passed the bar, I passed, I passed," I said.

"But you were sure you were going to fail," Mom squeaked.

"The bar professors advised us to say it to deter you from pestering us about the results. I passed."

Mom choked up. I hadn't been sure of passing and had prepared my parents for the possibility of failure. Her tears set mine off, too. Mom told me to call back in fifteen minutes to tell my dad, who had stepped out on an errand. She swore not to say anything.

When Dad answered the phone, he yelled, "Congratulations." I could hear the ice cubes clinking in his drink. He was a happy man.

My family traveled to D.C. for my swearing-in, which lasted less than ten minutes. Dad commented he didn't know of any other profession that congratulated its people so many times.

With my bar credentials under my belt, I had a new sense of confidence, and I knew what I wanted next: a judicial clerkship. I set the gears in motion. It was job-hunting time.

I interviewed for a clerkship with the Honorable Henry F. Greene in Washington, D.C., Superior Court. As I wheeled into the office for my interview, I saw a law clerk eating an apple with her feet up on the desk. Judge Greene walked by and commented on her hard work. The clerk replied, "Eat rocks, Harry."

I was shocked but recovered as the friendly banter continued amid laughter and smiles. For my first job in the legal profession, I worked as a judicial law clerk to Judge Greene, a.k.a. Harry. He was assigned to the traffic court when I first arrived and then, later, to the misdemeanor trial section. I enjoyed attending court, watching the trials, and speaking with him.

On my first day on the job, I brought a large bin of chocolate cookies I had baked. I had heard the judge adored chocolate. He was thrilled. Later the same day, he summoned me to his office, told me the cookies were delicious, and invited me to try one before they were all gone. I declined. He said, "I have a dilemma," and explained his wife and kids were likely to be upset if he didn't bring some cookies home. Then he stopped, thought a minute, and said, "I guess I can get over that." He proceeded to eat the remainder of the cookies. It was going to be a fun year.

Harry and I were both new at our jobs, so it was a time of learning and growing for both of us. My experience as his clerk whetted my appetite for trial work, so I applied to be an Assistant United States Attorney (AUSA). The AUSAs are the prosecutors for crimes committed in the District of Columbia. They decide who and what crimes to charge, investigate the crimes, and take the cases to trial.

I was rejected for the job on my first attempt. Undaunted, I applied again close to the end of my term with Harry, and this time I was successful.

TRAVEL HIGHS AND EXALTED COMPANY

I had a few months gap before my starting date as Assistant U.S. Attorney. It was 1982. Figuring I might not have this amount of free time again for a long while, I decided to embrace my dream of traveling around the world. I was up for the challenge.

I plotted the trip for months and saved every spare penny — thrift had always been my strong point. I learned it was possible to travel around the world on one ticket on a deal offered by several airlines, provided you kept going in one direction, with no backtracking. I found a deal including Australia, allowing me to visit my friends there.

No one else I knew was available to travel with me, so I prepared to travel alone — my itinerary: Paris, Rome, Bangkok, Hong Kong, Sydney, and Honolulu.

I stopped in New Jersey first to visit my parents. I remember my dad saying, "This will be the trip of a lifetime."

I mumbled, "Yeah, one of them."

I flew from New York to Paris, where I had arranged a rental car. Unfortunately, neither the car nor my luggage arrived on time, so I booked into an airport hotel and slept. The next day, my luggage and car were both delivered.

It was a four-door, not two as I had requested. Which meant I could not stow my chair in the usual way. Instead, I had to enter through the passenger side, throw my leg over the console, and then clear some space on the passenger seat, where I heaved the folded chair into the passenger compartment. I dragged myself over the console into the driver's seat and then pulled the rest of the chair into the passenger area. Once done, I had to stretch to reach the passenger door to close it.

The process was exhausting and took about ten minutes. It persuaded me to switch my itinerary to driving more and getting in and out of the car less.

The hand controls were different from those of my car back home and took some getting used to. There was a knob mounted on the column for braking. Another knob on the wheel for steering and a circular bar mounted on top of the steering wheel to accelerate. The handbrake was a separate push-down handle on the right. This meant when I wanted to reverse or shift gears I had to use my left hand for the handle on the right so I could shift with the gears on the console. It was all quite awkward, but hey, it worked.

The original plan was to stay in France for about a week to ten days. I wanted to see how carefree and spontaneous I could be. I hit the road with no plan or reservations, just my trusty Michelin guide to tell me where the accessible hotels were.

I decided to leave Paris for the end of the trip and headed north to Rouen. This was the city known for its famous citizen, Joan of Arc. According to my guidebook, there was an accessible motel nearby.

Driving in my first French city with a new car and equipment, no French, and ignorant of the road signs was dumb and scarier than I had imagined. I found myself driving in circles, irritating many. I found the hotel and felt lucky to be alive.

I simply had to see Mont Saint-Michel. After hours of driving, I finally spotted it in the distance. But when I approached the supposedly accessible hotel, I saw it was a motel, and all the rooms faced the parking lot. Each one had the same type of entrance, which was up one step through a very skinny door. This was not how I defined accessible, and it was not going to work. I drove on to the parking lot outside of Mont Saint-Michel, looked at the entrance to the site, and realized it was not going to work either. I appreciated the view for a few minutes and decided it best to find a hotel before dark, so I headed toward the next city I could find on the map, Rennes.

By the time I arrived, I was exhausted.

My guidebook indicated there were hotels in the center of town. I followed the signs and found one that on the outside appeared cozy. I parked, checked in, and was pleasantly surprised by my room.

I was also famished. I went to the hotel restaurant to order some food but couldn't read the French menu, so I had to guess. It was 1981. I'd been advised not to drink water or eat uncooked food. When my order was delivered, it was a cold salad. I was afraid to eat it.

As I had boarded the plane in New York to depart on this adventure, my wise mother had said: If they sell duty-free liquor, you might buy a bottle of brandy. You never know when it might come in handy. I went to my room and introduced myself to Cognac. We soon became well acquainted, but purely for medicinal purposes of course.

After some soul-searching, I decided spontaneity was both scary and anxiety-provoking when alone in a foreign country.

This was not fun, and I missed people. The next day I hit the high-way straight to Paris, found a comfortable room at a Novotel, and started calling all the phone numbers people had given me for friends they knew in Paris. Many didn't pick up, but then things started improving.

Steven and Esther Powellson answered my call. They were friends of my elderly next-door neighbor back in D.C. They in-sisted on taking me to dinner. We went to a charming restaurant called Le Soufflé, and as the name suggests, there was a wide selection of delicious soufflés to choose from.

For work reasons, Steve and Esther had been living near Paris for decades. Now approaching retirement, they were delighted to entertain. Steven had an interesting side hobby: He was memoriz-ing the *Iliad*, in Ancient Greek. He later gave talks describing how it was meant to be a spoken poem. The audience was encouraged to challenge him by asking for a phrase or supplying one and having him complete it in either Greek or English. He had it down cold.

Esther soon adopted me. She would call in the morning and say, "Have you been to the Pompidou Center yet?" Or "Did you know there is a free flute concert at the church tonight?" We took long strolls together. Over the years, I returned many times to this amazing city and visited Steve and Esther whenever I could.

The next day, I ventured forth in my chair and began on the Left Bank, where I could roll along, window-shop, and soak in the ambiance. But then hunger called. I searched for a restaurant or café with a flat entrance. I entered a little deli, only to find a big freezer blocking the path to the seating area. I began to back out, but the shop owners saw me and hurried over. They insisted I stay and with the help of some other customers, physically pushed the huge freezer out of my way. With great aplomb, they then directed me to a table and delivered the menu. I felt a bit flustered by all the commotion I had caused but grateful for their kindness. I ordered a chicken sandwich and a Coke. It was the best bread, chicken, and Coke I had ever eaten, and I enjoyed it thoroughly despite a huge cockroach scampering across the table as it was delivered. When it was time to leave, the shopkeepers waved goodbye as if to an old friend.

I left Paris and headed for Rome via Frankfurt on Lufthansa Airlines. I was traveling alone, but my mother was due to join me in Rome in a few days. Arriving in Frankfurt, I was placed in an ambulance and driven to the airport from our landing on the tarmac. Once we arrived at the terminal, I was lifted into one of the airport wheelchairs and taken on a winding path through the bowels of the building. It felt like a maze or labyrinth. My guide knocked on a heavy door, and it opened. I was pushed into a small room where many other people in wheelchairs were sitting. They lifted their heads to see who had come in but did not speak. The room was quiet. As my wheelchair pusher turned to leave, I asked what was happening. A woman appeared from behind the desk and said the attendant would come back for me when my flight was ready. I began to talk with one of the young men there in a wheelchair. He had no further information. Finally, I asked if I could go up to the main part of the airport. I was told I could not leave until the doctor cleared me.

Shortly thereafter, a doctor and his assistant arrived. They told me I could not board my next flight without medical clearance. Before leaving home, I had anticipated something like this. I had my home doctor prepare a letter stating I was a traumatic paraplegic and was not ill. He listed my medications and said I was safe to travel. I explained to the doctor I was not ill, just paralyzed. He said it was not good enough and I needed a medical exam costing fifty German marks. I could not leave without it. I declined.

As the time for my flight approached, I grew increasingly concerned. I asked the head warden if I could speak with the top manager or head of the office. She replied, "Of course, but you understand she is busy and will not be able to see you until after the flight leaves." I detected a hint of a satisfied smile.

I asked to see the doctor again. He returned with his assistant. I said, "I don't have fifty German marks, and you won't allow me upstairs to the airport proper to go to a bank to withdraw the money. I am not sick, merely paralyzed, and I have a letter from my doctor to confirm it."

The warden grabbed the letter, glanced at it, said, "Not good enough," and threw it back at me. The assistant looked apologetic but was not in charge. As the warden began repeating the requirements for my freedom, I felt like I wanted to cry in frustration. My inner voice said, *Don't let them see you cry*. But another inner voice nagged, *Patti, she is German, you are part German, you know she will not break the rigid rules. You need to cry to escape from the rules*. And so, I let myself cry. I was so frustrated; it was easy. I started wailing and saying, "I'm not sick, don't have fifty German marks, I'm forbidden to go to a bank, and I have a doctor's letter." I continued, rubbing my teary eyes and looking as sad as I could.

The warden became flustered. The assistant became flustered. The doctor became flustered. The doctor grabbed my letter and said, "How about if I just say this is good enough and sign it as approved?"

I nodded a tearful yes. But what I was thinking was, *No shit, Sherlock* as I dramatically dabbed my eyes one more time.

The doctor approved my letter and safe status, and the airline folks couldn't get me out of there fast enough. They lifted me into a waiting ambulance and sped to the airplane. I was the last person aboard. They were holding the plane for me. As I entered, a sleek flight attendant with a welcoming smile said, "Glad you could make it."

After the difficult layover in Frankfurt, my next stop was Rome. I had reservations at a Holiday Inn there, on the outskirts of the town, where my mom was to join me in a few days. On the night of my arrival in Rome, I received a phone call.

A friend had introduced me, via a letter, to the Reverend Jan Schotte, who lived and worked at the Vatican. Father Schotte was originally from Belgium and had begun his religious journey as a missionary. He spoke nine languages and worked closely with Pope John XXIII.

Father Scotty, as he became known to me, arrived at my hotel to take me to a restaurant for dinner. He wedged me into his tiny VW bug, and we headed toward the city. As we drove down the main street, I saw a view of the Vatican backlit by the sunset and gasped.

"Have you never seen it before?" he asked.

"No," I said.

"Then what are we waiting for?"

He drove straight onto the cobblestones of the Vatican Plaza, stopping near a large obelisk. He dragged my wheelchair out of his tiny car, helped me get seated, turned me around, and let me see it all. He pointed out the interesting details, including his balcony and the Pope's window.

I'll never forget a story he told me: Installing the obelisk in the center of the pavilion in front of St. Peter's had presented a huge problem. To raise the obelisk into place, workers had encircled the heavy stone monument, each holding a strong rope attached to the top. Together, they hauled it upward toward its final standing position. Unfortunately, they hit a snag when they discovered the ropes were a few inches too short to raise the obelisk to a vertical position. After much debate about what to do, one of the engineers had a brilliant idea.

At this point, Father Scotty paused. This reverent, God-fearing monsignor of the church, who worked closely with the Pope and was standing on hallowed grounds, stood with his hand over his mouth, stifling a giggle.

"The men," he explained, eyes gleaming with mirth, "were commanded to piss on the ropes. As a result, the ropes stretched just enough to finish the job. It was a miracle."

With the history lesson concluded and a good laugh, we went to dinner.

Father Scotty suggested my mother and I shouldn't lodge so far out of the city and kindly invited us to stay at his apartment in the Vatican. The apartment had two extra bedrooms and a small chapel. Mom and I sent loads of postcards home saying we'd moved in with a priest at the Vatican.

Father Scotty gave us a personal tour of the Vatican. As we exited the church, several women walking by reached out and touched my sleeve. I almost didn't notice, but Father pointed it out to me. He said the women were touching me purposely and reverentially as they walked by. He explained that according to the Catholic faith, people with disabilities were specially chosen by God. The women wanted to touch the chosen person.

For me, this was a new view of being physically challenged, and I decided to embrace it.

Father Scotty obtained tickets for my mother and me to attend an outdoor papal audience. I told him, respectfully, that I hoped the seats weren't in a handicapped section, as I preferred being treated like everyone else. He nodded.

My mom was thrilled. We were a Catholic family for generations. My parents and I had attended Catholic schools. Catholicism was not just a religion to us. It was a set of values and a culture, with all its traditions and quirks.

Father Scotty warned us thousands of others would be present at the papal audience, but we weren't concerned. On the appointed day, we showed our tickets to the Swiss Guard, who, to my disappointment, guided us to seats in the handicapped section.

Pope John XXIII greeted each person in the section individually. My mom cried when she met His Reverence. Recalling what

I had been taught in Catholic grammar school, I kissed his ring and said, "It's a pleasure to meet you."

The Pope looked at me quizzically.

"It's a pleasure to meet you," I repeated.

"Ah, Napoli, Napoli," the Pope replied after a moment.

The American next to me leaned over and said, "You talk too fast. He thinks you're from Naples."

So much for my big moment.

Later, I told Father Scotty we had been seated in the wheelchair section. He listened intently and asked me a few questions. A few months later, when my mom was looking at the tickets, she called me. She had noticed we had been assigned seats in the front row, not in the handicapped section. The Swiss Guard, seeing me in my wheelchair, had assumed I was to be seated there. The guard never even looked at my ticket. Father Scotty was cleared of responsibility for the error. He had heard my complaint and had never said a word in his defense.

My friendship with Father endured until his passing. I returned to Rome to see him, and we met when he came to the U.S. on papal business. On one occasion, he took me on a tour of the gardens at the Pope's villa at Palace Gandolfo. We stopped for lunch on the way back to Rome in a little, out-of-the-way village. At the restaurant, awaiting our food, we had an animated conversation about abortion and women's rights. At one point in the conversation, I realized we were a bit loud, so said, "Father, we better keep it down, or people will think something is going on between us."

He was dressed in a full cassock with his monsignor trimmings and a huge cross necklace. He smiled quietly and responded, "Honey, this is Italy. They are *sure* we are having an affair."

From Rome, I flew to Bangkok, Thailand. Tony, the son of my neighbor, was waiting for me at the terminal. He was working in Bangkok and had been informed about my arrival details by his mom. This was a true blessing, as I couldn't understand the unfamiliar alphabet signs or read directions.

He drove me to the hotel, and then we headed to the bar for a drink.

A beautiful Thai woman waited on us. I was awed by her elegance and poise. When she slowly poured the beer into the tall beer glasses, I was mesmerized. As she walked away, I thought, *If I ever walk again — I want to walk like her.*

My first excursion in Bangkok was a temple tour, which included a boat trip on the *klongs* (canals). When the tour was set to begin, a large motorbus pulled up to the front of the hotel. The tour guide emerged. She was a petite Thai woman. She looked at me and, in a panicky voice, said, "You aren't on this tour, are you?"

She was not pleased with my affirmative response.

"You can't get on this bus. I can't carry you on this bus. How will you get on the bus?" she blurted.

"Someone will help," I responded (willing it to happen).

She repeated, almost wailing, "I can't help you on this bus."

An English-speaking gentleman approached and said he was happy to help. Another angel to the rescue. He carried me on and off the bus at each stop, and he helped me into the boat on the *klongs*. I appreciated his efforts, which were kind and not patronizing. From the boat, we saw many aspects of life on the waterways: fresh produce, as well as any other product you could want, piled on boats for sale — even a large stack of empty coffins. We visited a snake farm. My helper transported me safely and enthusiastically to each spot.

I arrived in Hong Kong late in the evening and was hungry. After securing my belongings in my hotel room, I went out to the street to find a place to eat. The hotel I was staying in only had one restaurant, and it was German-themed. I have nothing against German food, but it was not what I had come to Hong Kong to eat.

I strolled the streets and absorbed the wonderful energy and apparent chaos. There were neon signs everywhere, some on top of others, filling the streets with lights and colors. There were so many signs and neon lights it was dazzling and hard to pinpoint a particular building. With their lights, noise, confusion, and controlled chaos, the streets of Hong Kong were like being inside a huge video game. There seemed to be neither rhyme nor reason to the street patterns.

Masses of people were walking on the sidewalks, and the streets were jammed with noisy bumper-to-bumper traffic and blaring horns. As I took it all in, I could not help grinning from ear to ear. I began my search for a wheelchair-accessible restaurant but soon realized my prospect of finding one was not good. I was not too interested in the few accessible shops suspending chicken and beef carcasses from the ceiling in full view through the window. The more sedate, appealing places, the ones with food not swinging in the air, had steps down to their entrances.

I looked around to see if I could make eye contact and find someone to help me. But people avoided me and avoided my looks. Every time I approached someone, they looked down at the ground and walked away. Finally, I realized I was not only hungry but lost.

I began to look for people who might be English-speaking. Seeing two tall Caucasians walking by, I yelled, "Excuse me, do you speak English?" They stopped, looked at one other, and answered, "Yes, we speak English. What do you need?"

With some relief, I asked, "Do you know where the Holiday Inn is? I seem to have lost it."

The tall, blond Englishman said, "Hmm, do you mean *that* Holiday Inn?" pointing directly across the street.

I felt foolish, but John and his companion, Pete, would have none of it. They insisted on escorting me to the hotel and began to push me across the road. They were jovial and talkative, and we had a conversation going in no time. In front of the hotel, we talked for a while. I learned John and Pete were natives of Manchester, England, enjoying a brief vacation from their current jobs in Saudi Arabia.

Finally, Pete asked, "Why were you on the street anyway?" I explained I had been looking for a restaurant. When they learned I was still hungry, the evening truly began. John, Pete, and I ended up visiting three restaurants.

We hired a bicycle rickshaw, and Pete jumped in. One advantage of my wheelchair life is I have developed extraordinarily strong arms. I grabbed hold of the back of the rickshaw, and John jumped onto the back of my wheelchair. We crossed the main road, stopping traffic, looking like a circus act. The rickshaw driver was initially not too pleased with us, but after we gave him a generous tip, he smiled. We had a joyful time and spent the following days touring together.

My next stop was Sydney, Australia, for a reunion with my Australian family from my high school days. The Bryants had moved to a seaside community. They had set up a bed for me in the first-floor dining room and rigged a shower in their laundry room. I had washed and slept in stranger places. It worked quite well.

We shared family dinners, day trips, and talks over tea. It was relaxing to stroll through the area, do a little shopping, and spend downtime with my Aussie family. I loved riding the ferries past the opera house and to the beach.

Just like my previous visit, this one was truly restorative. Once again, it was difficult to leave my Australian friends and family.

Next up was Honolulu. I drove all around the island and wheeled everywhere. I picked up a guidebook and stopped at all the suggested locations, including the best surfing beaches and the touristy Hawaiian Village. I loved strolling along the sidewalk on the beach in Waikiki and watching the evening sun slip down into the ocean. I loved Hawaii's sweet-scented air and felt amazingly free and comfortable.

The three-day stop had given me time to pause, take in all my experiences, and reboot for my next phase of life: the new job.

For eight weeks, I'd been terrified, rescued, experienced delightful adventures, and met fabulous people. Following my return to D.C. and a few days back in the old routine, I suffered from mild depression. I understood the problem. On the trip, every day presented new challenges. I relished the challenges and figuring out how to overcome them. The experiences had taken me away from some of the tedium associated with life in a wheelchair. Now, I was missing the challenge and the difference in culture. On my trip, I was free to be me and to experience the different ways in which people with a disability were regarded. The truth was, I did not like the way people like me were regarded in the United States. Leaving and returning had highlighted the differences. I felt ungrounded.

In hindsight, I shouldn't have worried. It was naïve of me to think there were no challenges back in the U.S.

I have continued my love of travel and added numerous other destinations, including Phuket, Phnom Penh, and Angkor Wat in Cambodia, where I managed to snag my first elephant ride. Touring the temples was awe-inspiring. The architecture and art were stunning and powerful. But on the personal side, all along the way, people jumped in to help push me, lift me, or rescue me and make sure I saw it all.

I've visited Singapore and New Zealand and been breathless at Lake Titicaca in Bolivia (at 12,500 feet altitude) and much of Central and South America. I have participated in international bilateral negotiations in several South American countries, made presentations in the Caribbean Islands, Central America, and Malaysia, joined an international money-laundering policy conference in France, and directed money-laundering risk assessments and reports in Ecuador and Guatemala.

I have learned to access vehicles from rickshaws to buses and have even been strapped onto a motorcycle with bungee cords. I have taken showers and used restrooms in creative ways, from piles of pillows making a chair in the tub to handheld showers in the middle of the open bathroom floor. I have learned the value of a handheld shower when a bathroom tub is inaccessible and how to make do with just a sink when necessary. I let people know when I need help — and exactly what and how to decline firmly when I don't.

Most people act surprised to see me traveling alone. After the initial shock, though, they usually give me a supportive grin or a thumbs-up. If I am pushing myself up a steep hill or ramp, strangers frequently run to my assistance spontaneously. If I get to the top of a hill without their help, I often get applause. I have learned to embrace downhills, in which I take immense pleasure — I roll as fast as I can, with my arms outstretched, feeling the breeze and the sense of freedom it brings. Passers-by often stop, smile, and nod their appreciation. But there are the worriers, too, who insist on pushing me to wherever I am going next, whether I want them to or not. Suddenly, my chair will take up a life or a speed of its own, and I realize someone has taken the handles behind me and decided to drive.

My journeys have been as much about seeing places and cultures as seeing the true nature, kindness, and commonalities in people. In Bangladesh, a small girl of about ten approached me. She carried a mobility-impaired child on her hip, slung in a large shawl fastened around her neck. She was fascinated by my chair.

The young girl asked me where she could get a chair like mine for her little brother.

In Angkor Wat, Cambodia, a small child of two or three was assisting an older woman in tending to an altar in the temple. The child herself was barefoot, as was the old woman, and they both wore tattered, simple garments. They continued to tend to the altar, placing flowers and incense and kept an eye on me. As I waited for my friends, who had gone to another inaccessible part of the temple, the old woman called the little girl over to her. After they conversed briefly, the child approached me shyly. After I smiled and greeted her, she handed me a small packet of money. In Cambodia, among the countless beggars, the most successful ones were physically impaired. The child and her guardian, barefoot and in tattered clothes, felt sorry for me. I was touched but also confused. I didn't feel I could accept their money, yet I didn't want to offend them. I returned the packet to the little girl with a smile, and I bowed my head to her and her guardian. I hoped I was not insulting them. Because their actions had been prompted by pure, genuine emotions, I was not insulted. There is an enormous difference between compassion and sympathy, and theirs had been an act of compassion.

Over the years, the goodness in people has manifested itself in many ways. They want to do something for me, either to help or to make me smile. It took me time to accept this. Initially, I thought I had to prove how tough I was, but eventually, I realized I only had to prove my toughness to myself. After such a realization, I was able to gracefully accept the kindness of strangers. It has led to some wonderful moments. On many occasions, people have explained that they have a mobility-impaired person in their lives. They asked for my advice on how to handle a particular situation or inquired about my wheelchair and where to get one like it.

Just as people go out of their way for me, I like to give back. So, when the Secret Service decided to create a special entrance, with no tickets required, for people with a disability to tour the White House, I stepped right up, so to speak. Before 9/11, I was permitted to take up to four people with me on a tour and could go at any of the posted public times without reservation. I have taken many friends and visitors on White House tours.

Throughout my career, I have had the privilege to meet many distinguished government officials, including President Ronald and First Lady Nancy Reagan, President Bill and First Lady Hillary Clinton, and Secretary-General of the United Nations Kofi Anan. Throughout my nomination process and during my nomination hearing, I met Iowa's Senator Harkin, the sponsor of the America with Disabilities Act. I've had the privilege of testifying before several U.S. senators on Capitol Hill. But my real heroes were Justices of the Supreme Court. For a while, Sandra Day O'Connor and I lived in the same building, and I later moved into the same condominium complex as Ruth Bader Ginsburg. (She and I even worked out in the gym together one time.)

My travels and life experiences have taught me to see the unique beauty and ability in each person and to relish the challenges of adjusting to new experiences and circumstances. Unfortunately, this view is not universally held, so I have had a lot of informal teaching to do.

LEARNING TO BE A PROSECUTOR

Being appointed as an assistant U.S. attorney (AUSA) to the Criminal Division was the beginning of the rest of my life. All I wanted to do was to try cases before a jury; I had applied to both the prosecutor's office as well as the Public Defender Service. I appreciated the roles of both sides, and I was happy for either. As it turned out, the U.S. Attorney's office was willing to take a chance on the lawyer in the wheelchair.

I started in the Office's Criminal Division, which was split into sections for Misdemeanors, Appellate, Homicide, Grand Jury, Felony, and so on. Technically, I had the knowledge and confidence to do the job, but I was anxious to put my courtroom skills to the test. I had hoped to begin in the Misdemeanor Section, the usual route for newcomers. However, my first assignment turned out to be in the Appellate Section, which is where cases are heard on appeal from the Trial Court.

Although legal rules apply to each circumstance, a party who is unhappy with the outcome of a court case may appeal it in the Appellate Section. I was terrified to begin my legal career there since the work involves detailed research and report writing, not oral advocacy, and therefore, not the sharpest elements of my skillset.

After a verdict, the defendant typically finds some avenue to appeal. In a criminal case, the government does not have the right to appeal except under exceptional circumstances. Losers in civil trial verdicts file appeals, hoping to change the outcome from the trial court. Once the appeal is filed in a government case, a government lawyer must file a response. These filings are called briefs — though they never are.

My assignment to the Appellate Section turned out to be an unexpected gift. Appeals are instigated for many reasons, including errors during a trial, bad procedures, poor decisions, evidence later proved incorrect, or statements turning out to be untrue.

During my time in the Appellate Section, reading trial transcripts and researching the issues presented, I learned great lessons about the things a lawyer should *not* do during a trial. Specifically, I learned about things a lawyer should *not* say in closing arguments, I became cognizant of diverse types of witness issues, and I observed examples of how to make a judge extremely furious.

It slowly dawned on me why supervisors had first assigned me to the Appellate Section and not Misdemeanors. In Appellate, the work was researching and writing — not presenting cases in court. Although I had been hired as an AUSA, the authorities weren't convinced I could handle an actual trial in court. Thankfully, I wouldn't be stuck there in perpetuity.

Each lawyer was expected to rotate through several sections of the U.S. Attorney's office. The first was usually the Misdemeanor Section, followed by the Grand Jury Section, the Appellate Section, and the Felony Section. I was the only prosecutor required to shadow another colleague for a day. I discovered the higher-ups' main concern: The AUSA's transferred case files, often masses of paperwork, to the courtroom on big, heavy carts. The bosses worried I could not physically manage the carts and the accompanying logistics.

This made me angry, but it also made me laugh. I had been pushing grocery carts in my wheelchair for some time now, so there was no logistical issue. In truth, I was quite deft. It's too bad pushing carts wasn't an Olympic sport.

But the other reality was that I never had to push any cart, thanks to the inherent kindness of fellow human beings. Whenever someone saw me struggling with many files or a cart, they offered to help, especially the police officer witnesses. No, carts and papers were not my problem. The people who assumed carts caused me difficulties were the problem. Their rationale demonstrated a lack of understanding and a reluctance to consult me about it for fear of appearing less than all-knowing. People can be much harder to navigate than steps or carts.

Once I eventually rotated to the Misdemeanor Division, I discovered the training for trials was based on the method of baptism by fire. First, you watched your slightly more experienced colleague handle a trial, and then it was your turn.

My colleague's example was a search warrant case, where the police had gone into a home with a warrant to seize drugs. They had seized enough drug packages to fill a portable freezer about three feet long. The hostile defense attorney admitted that even Jesus Christ would be convicted with all those drugs.

My first solo trial was the case of a young man who had gone to a nightclub. No seats were available, so when a customer stood up to buy a drink, the defendant stole their seat. When the customer returned, the defendant refused to give up the seat, and words were exchanged. As the customer left in defeat, the defendant rose from the stolen seat and bit him on the back of his neck, leaving permanent tooth marks. The defendant had been charged with assault.

The defendant decided to testify on his behalf. On cross-examination, he admitted he trained dogs and preferred animals to people. In the closing argument, I suggested to the jury this experience must have led to his dog-biting behavior. The jury was out for only sixteen minutes before convicting him.

In another case, a young man had gone into the accounting office at a local university to repair some machines. When he finished his tasks, he had the office manager sign his job order sheet, confirming the work had been completed. As he walked through the lobby on his way out, a large red cloud began to form around his hand. When he realized what was going on, he threw the object in his hand away and ran out the door.

In the accounting office, the cashiers each had a top drawer with a fake pile of money in it. The top bill was real, but it was attached to a stack of fake bills — which was a red dye pack. In the event someone removed what they thought to be a package of bills from the drawer, it activated the dye pack in a few minutes, and a red cloud formed when making their escape.

The defendant managed to escape but had left his signed work order, splashed with red dye, on the floor with the remains of the dye pack. The defendant was not interested in accepting a plea offer and insisted on going to trial. Just before the trial, I asked the defense attorney what his client's defense would be. He told me he didn't know but then added, "If you mention to the jury that he was caught red-handed, I will object." The defendant was found guilty.

One day, I was sitting in the lobby waiting for the court to open when a defense attorney came up to me. He was extremely thin, tall, stooped, and looked ancient. His shock of pure white hair was the only energetic thing about him. I provided him with the name of the AUSA who was assigned to try his case, to which he responded, "I'm glad it's not you."

"Why?" I asked.

"The jury is likely to feel sorry for you because of the wheelchair, and I would lose."

"Then, I'm so pleased I am not trying your case," I said.

"Why?" he said.

"The jury might feel sorry for you because of your age, and then I would lose." He hobbled away with a sound somewhere between a harrumph and a grunt.

One day, I had a particularly thorny case. Not much evidence was going my way. During the lunch break, I went to a supervisor to ask for advice. He "pumped me up" with a few ideas and lots of encouragement. Fortified, I returned to the courtroom to try it all out.

I lost the case. I returned to the supervisor and told him about it.

"Of course you did," he said. "The case was a 'dog.' But you needed the experience."

It was the early 1980s. Bumper stickers on cars shared sentiments such as *I'd rather be sailing, I'd rather be golfing,* or *I'd rather be at the beach.* I pasted a bumper sticker on the back of my chair saying, *I'd rather be dancing.* I loved the way it made people laugh and relax around me.

Before one of my trials, the defense attorney approached the court with a motion requesting the court to have the sticker removed from the back of my wheelchair, where the jury could see it as I moved around the courtroom.

"Why?" the judge asked.

"Because it is a form of communication with the jury," the defense attorney responded.

"That's all you have?" said the judge. "Motion denied."

After the Misdemeanor Section, I was assigned to the Grand Jury Section. It gathered evidence, directed investigations on felony cases, and then presented its findings to the grand jury. The jury voted as to whether there was probable cause to charge and who to charge.

It was fascinating because, unlike in normal jury trials, there is no defense attorney; the jurors themselves ask the witnesses questions. Listening to what they asked was a revelation in learning how people think and react to evidence, as well as in appreciating the types of evidence they want to hear. It was a master class in appreciating matters a jury needs to hear, even things legally irrelevant, such as intent or motive in a case not legally requiring proof of either. It's why, most of the time, prosecutors only bring cases they think they can win to the grand jury. Juries have a reputation for being extraordinarily unpredictable.

In one case, a young woman had become pregnant by her boyfriend and had given birth to a little boy. However, she later decided to split with him out of concern for her and her child's safety. When she decided to leave him, the boyfriend became even more physically abusive. Concerned, the young woman went to court and was awarded a protective order requiring the now ex-boyfriend to stay at least one hundred feet away from her, the child, and their apartment.

One day, the defendant came around, allegedly to visit the child on his birthday. He pushed in the apartment door, shoved her into the bedroom, and threw her onto the bed. He raped and physically assaulted her. He then dressed her and pulled her out of the apartment and into the elevator. In the elevator, she was convinced he was going to kill her. Somehow, she managed to convince him to let her make a phone call from the lobby office to arrange for someone to take care of their son. Instead, she contacted the police, who arrived in moments. They arrested the defendant and found his Stay Away/Protection order in his pocket.

The grand jury heard the case and listened to the dramatic statement by the young woman. They believed her version of the events, yet they voted not to charge the defendant, explaining they didn't get involved in family matters. In 1984, domestic violence was not a familiar term in the lexicon. Rape and physical assault were still family matters.

I was horrified, almost speechless. Finally, incredulously, I asked the jurors, "What is she supposed to do? Are you saying she should lie down and be raped whenever he comes by?" They had no answer. I was stunned and felt rage bubbling up inside. It did not get any better when I tried to discuss it with the supervisors, who were all white men. It was truly an eye-opening experience. I took a big gulp to absorb the anger and promised myself not to give up on these types of cases.

Gradually, I progressed through career rotation to the Felony Trial Section. The heavy caseload mostly involved drugs, guns, and the occasional serious assault and/or robbery. We received cases indicted by the Grand Jury Section and had to meet the witnesses and prepare the cases for trial. When we went to trial, we made opening statements, presented and questioned our witnesses, and questioned or cross-examined any defense witnesses. Finally, we made closing arguments.

At one point, after I had about sixteen trials under my belt, I was called into the Felony Section chief's office to discuss my annual review. The chief was sitting in a relaxed manner behind his desk, wearing a kindly, patronizing smile, as he handed me a copy of my first evaluation. I looked at it and was dismayed to see the smiling chief had given me mediocre grades. I inquired as to what I had done to deserve such a poor appraisal.

The chief did not offer specifics. Instead, he told me the inadequacy of my experience to date was the problem. Given more trials, I would improve. He smiled broadly as he leaned over the desk with a paternal smile and condescending expression.

"Is this the only grade achievable at my level of experience?" I asked.

"No," he said.

"Then how can I improve the evaluation at my level of experience?"

"It's hard to say."

"Is it my writing?"

"No."

"Is it my courtroom work?"

"No."

"Are others at my level of experience being awarded different grades? Can you tell me what they do differently?"

"Can't say. It's just what we've heard about you."

"From the judges I appear before?"

"No."

"Then from whom?"

"Can't say, specifically."

"Can you tell me what to do to get a better evaluation?"

"No."

My questions continued until my allotted hour was up. By the time I was ready to leave, the chief was seated with his back against the wall, arms, and legs crossed tightly. He wasn't grinning anymore as he passed me the appraisal form with a pen.

"Should I sign this?" I asked.

"Yes."

"Does signing it mean I agree with it?"

"No, you can go to the head guy and discuss it if you don't agree with it."

"Okay, then I will sign it with the understanding I will be going to the head guy." I signed it and left.

I went directly to the office of the chief of the Felony Trial Section, the person who made all the rotation assignments. I scheduled an appointment with him through his secretary. Then I went into my office, closed the door, and called my dad, upset and crying. I broke down and told him everything.

Dad told me, "You did good, honey. Now, have a good cry, go to the restroom, put cold water on those eyes, and go back to work."

Which is what I did.

I was hard at work when, a few minutes later, I heard a knock on my door. The Felony Chief walked in and said, "I thought about our discussion. I'm going to contact some of the judges you appeared before and then revisit your evaluation."

"Thank you," I said.

He changed my evaluation to "Outstanding." He figured out that even though I was in a wheelchair, I knew how to question a witness and make my point.

During my time in the Felony Section, I prosecuted between fifty and sixty felonies in jury trials. One was a robbery case. Two defendants, one male and one female (who sported a big gold tooth with a diamond in it), had gone into Murray's steak store. This was a chain store selling meat cuts. Inside, there were aisles of freezers filled with steaks and meat options — nothing fancy, just the product.

The two defendants had entered the steak store, gone up to the freezer containing the best and most expensive steaks, and then began removing piles of them. When approached by a salesperson, the male defendant threatened the employee with a scowl and an intimidating stare. Then, he and his partner just walked out with the steaks and drove away. They hit three separate locations of Murray's steak stores in one day.

Some of the store employees testified. They had all, but especially the males, felt frightened of the defendants, and they demonstrated how they had felt. One explained how he approached the male defendant with confidence and a can of beans in each hand. He then ducked behind the witness box to show what he did after the defendant spoke to him. His fear and panic were palpable.

The defense presented its case. All the defendants' witnesses gave the same alibi for the defendants: They had attended a birthday party with the defendants on the night of the robberies, and therefore, they said, the defendants couldn't have been robbing the store. However, on cross-examination, all the witnesses said they remembered the party because of the delicious food. I asked the witnesses whether beef had been served. When each defense witness answered with a hearty yes and noted they had enjoyed a superb grilled steak at the party, the defendants' lawyer just shook his head in disbelief. The jury found the defendants guilty.

Another trial was a co-defendant murder case. A young man walked into a parking lot, a known drug market, carrying a large television set he hoped to sell to buy some drugs. Unfortunately, he owed money to the defendant, a drug seller, who was not pleased to see him. The defendant yelled out, "Who wants a hundred dollars to off this man?" The co-defendant appeared from a doorway and said, "I do." He then picked up a baseball bat leaning against the building. He walked over to the young man with the TV set and slammed him in the head with the bat, killing him instantly. Photos of the decedent showed a head half gone. It was sickening.

All the witnesses at the trial were drug users and scared of the defendants. But, as we often tell juries, life is easier with fifty bishops as witnesses, but they are not the usual characters hanging out in parking lots looking to score drugs.

The jury hung, eleven to one, for conviction because a juror refused to deliberate for religious reasons. At the retrial, the defendant who had offered the money was found guilty, and the defendant with the bat was found not guilty. The not-guilty defendant yelled out, "But I'm more guilty than he is." Another jury agreed about six months later when he was convicted of a separate murder.

The marshals insisted on accompanying me to the building's exit for my protection. But the weird thing was the defendants — and in all my other cases — never threatened me. They usually said hello and held the door open for me. I came to realize people who wanted to receive respect and dignity were willing to give it to others.

On another day, I returned to the office after losing a case. I was sitting by the elevator feeling a bit crestfallen. I was disappointed in the verdict, and my energy was sapped. My shoulders sagged, and my head was slightly bowed. One of the supervisors came into the lobby area, saw me, and said, "Pat, what's wrong?"

"I just lost my case," I replied.

"Pat, did you do the best you could?" he asked.

"Yes."

"Are you being paid next week?"

"Yes."

"Did you look good?"

"Yes," I said and grinned.

"What is the problem, Pat?"

I thought, *What a great attitude. He is right.* He reminded me I was only responsible for doing my part well. I was not responsible for others' decisions or destinies. This was to be my new philosophy.

In one of my last trials in the Felony Section, I prosecuted a murder case in which the victim had been shot from behind. When the bullet hit his spine, he was instantly paralyzed, and he died soon thereafter. I described it all in my closing argument. After the jury went out to deliberate, the defense attorney made a motion for a mistrial because, she said, I had used the word *paralyzed* in my argument. It attracted attention and sympathy; therefore, the case needed a new trial or a dismissal.

The judge appeared incredulous.

He asked me whether I wished to respond. I said I did. I reminded the judge that *paralyzed* was an everyday word, and I was not prohibited from using it. I also pointed out that although I was in a wheelchair, no one on the jury knew why. They didn't know whether I was paralyzed, simply weak, or had a broken leg or two. The judge denied the motion with a look of faint disgust directed at the defense attorney.

I thought it was funny. In a strange way, the defense attorney had tried to use my paraplegia to win her case. I went back to my office to await the verdict when I spotted the big chief of the Criminal Division. He was responsible for managing all the different sections, e.g., misdemeanor, grand jury, felony, homicide, chronic offenders, etc. I went over and told him the story, thinking it might amuse him.

When I'd finished speaking, a look of panic spread over his face. Our senses of humor came from different planets. I sensed he feared I could not try any more cases with serious injuries, and all previous verdicts might be appealed.

Thankfully, his fears were short-lived because I did win the case.

I was next in line for rotation, which moved by seniority and competence, to be promoted to the Homicide Section in the office. This was the final step up — the highest rank — which not everyone who worked in the office achieved.

In the Homicide Section, cases were assigned directly to a prosecutor on intake. They saw the case through from the initial arrest to the end. We assessed the case, called in witnesses, and subpoenaed any relevant evidence. We then presented the case to the grand jury. When the grand jury voted to indict the case, the same prosecutor was responsible for preparing it and presenting it for trial. This procedure was called "vertical prosecution," and it was used in homicides and serious sexual offenses.

Some cases had no resolution.

An infant drowned in the bath, leaving no forensic evidence, differing witness stories, and no way to identify the exact person responsible. Many of the witnesses were terrified and regretted they had ever spoken up. They said they had forgotten what had happened. In frustration, I sometimes replied, "Hey, I am not dumb or blind, and I didn't get this job for my great legs, so let's get real."

This section handled cases of sexual abuse, and many included molested kids. It often turned out their moms had a history of being molested as a child. Frequently, the child's molester was the mother's boyfriend — who was waiting for them outside. Some of those cases did not go forward. The victims were trapped by their circumstances and too frightened of the perpetrator to press charges. How could they leave the breadwinner and put him in jail?

Every day, I saw the worst of humanity and the victims who had been left behind. Additionally, the justice system worked slowly, and it was difficult to feel as though any single person could truly make a difference or be a positive influence. The constant exposure to sadness and violence took its toll. Eventually, I became the depressing person at parties when people asked about my job. I could see the pain and the fear in the eyes of the witnesses, and I wanted to help ease it. However, as the prosecutor, I represented the citizens of the United States, specifically of the District of Columbia. I did not represent any individual witness or victim, and my resources to help were limited. I needed to earn the trust of the witnesses to have them present honestly and genuinely, and this frequently meant exploring and exposing their pain and frustration. It was difficult not to take some of their despair back onto myself. Additionally, I found, especially in homicide cases, families required answers for what happened to their loved ones. Many hoped the defendant would testify and explain everything. I felt pressure to try to help the families find closure — but it was a fruitless effort, and I found the job soul-destroying.

One day, I realized I was done. I could not change the circumstances of each case; I could only play my part, which I had done. It was time to seek a more positive place.

I accepted a position as a trial attorney at the Asset Forfeiture and Money Laundering Section of the Criminal Division of the U.S. Department of Justice.

My first assignment was a drug and asset forfeiture case in Cedar Rapids, Iowa. I was dispatched to Iowa to take over for two other Justice Department lawyers who did not have much trial experience. They were happy to take roles as co-counsel and let me do the talking, which has never been a problem for me.

When I entered the courtroom for the first time, the opposing lawyers stopped what they were doing and just up and stared at me. Initially, they registered surprise, then they smiled warmly, and then their smiles turned sly before morphing into arrogant sneers. I could almost hear them thinking, "Oh my god, is this all they have to go against us? What a cakewalk."

We were a bit disorganized during the jury selection and made some procedural errors. As a result, we could not eliminate as many of the potential jurors as we had hoped. This emboldened the defense team even further. Three defendants were represented by four attorneys, the best attorneys Iowa had to offer. The attorneys were feeling pumped after the jury was finally selected and opening statements began. I was seated with one colleague and was the only woman at the counsel table. The defense table, with its three defendants and four lawyers, was crowded.

In this case, the three defendants were well-known, well-to-do bachelors in a close-knit Midwestern town. Two owned some of the bars frequented by the college-age folks, and the third was a friend who socialized with them frequently. It became known they were partying with drugs, mainly cocaine, and sharing it freely with other young people at the clubs they owned, at their homes, and in their limousines. Many people in the community seemed to believe the defendants were untouchable; they were getting away with criminal behavior, and nothing could be done about it.

Coming into the case as an outsider from D.C., I was not appreciated by the locals. I went to a store and bought some pens and items reflecting the local college sports team to put on the counsel table to try to show a little humanity. Even so, I felt like an awkward outsider when opening statements began.

It's unusual to object during opening statements, but in this case, the defense counsel was taking things too far. In their opening statement to the jury, they inferred the case was a frame-up by the government and big city outsiders. I objected, and at the bench conference with the judge, I suggested the defense was trying to nullify the jury — which means to convince the jury to return a not guilty verdict, irrespective of their belief a defendant is guilty. (This is a rare and mostly unknown right of a jury. They, in effect, nullify a law they believe is immoral or wrongly applied to the defendant in the case.)

The lead counsel, Cedar Rapid's finest, with a mystified expression on his face, said, "What does she mean?"

"I'm well aware," said the judge. "And she is right. Objection sustained."

The momentum had swung in my favor.

The following day, a new female attorney from the lead defense lawyers firm came to sit at the counsel table. She lasted for a few days, just sitting there, showing the defense believed in women, too. But finally, she refused to return, and we were back to me and the guys.

It was a fascinating case involving defendants who owned various clubs, partied with young women, and partook in cocaine and whatever came with it. One of the defendants had a large, beautiful home where he invited young women into his bedroom to play on a little miniature golf green he had set up.

Originally, some of the women who had spent time with the defendants declined to appear as witnesses. I decided to call them to testify anyway. They were attractive young women who were inclined to be foolishly naïve. The defense had not expected me to call them up, and it was a most successful strategy because I knew how the testimony of these might affect the jury.

The defense had their hopes pinned on one witness. The original prosecutor had treated him cruelly, allegedly forcing him to lie about his friend's activities at the parties. After his witness conference with the prosecutors and giving evidence implicating his friends, he became ill, vomiting in the parking lot. The witness claimed it was caused by the allegedly terrifying experience with the cruel prosecutor.

The defense attorneys hoped the prosecutors would call this witness to testify against his friends. They could then cross-examine him on the horrors of the original prosecutor's behavior and show how the government was forcing false testimony.

I knew the defense would not rest until they heard from this witness, so I purposely did not call him as a witness. I decided I wanted to be the one to cross-examine him, as one could be much freer and use leading questions on cross-examination. As a prosecutor, I was familiar with the techniques used with witnesses, and I had also interviewed the prosecutor who had originally questioned the witness.

The strategy worked. The defense called the witness to make their point. However, because the witness was a defense witness, their questioning had to be limited and straightforward. I had more freedom in the form of the questions I was permitted to ask. On my cross-examination, the witness conceded he became ill because he had flipped or given evidence against his friends, not because of the actions of the government attorney. As for the allegedly cruel prosecutor, well, he had tossed his legal pad onto the desk with a loud noise, which had scared the witness. "I guess you had to be there," he mumbled when I replicated the action.

The defense attorneys looked stunned and bewildered at the end of the questioning. They were silent and unsmiling. I sensed they had finally realized they had played into the prosecutors' hands.

In Iowa, lawyers do not stand when they speak before the court; they remain seated. In D.C., when they want to speak, lawyers stand up to signal they have something to say. Naturally, I was unable to use this formal procedure in D.C., so I learned to interrupt when I wanted to speak. The tactic was accepted and worked well in D.C., but it was not welcome in Iowa, where I just had to politely wait my turn. I had some adjusting to do.

The trial took about seven weeks. It was one of the top three news stories of the year in Iowa. Every day, the press summarized the previous day's events, sensationalizing when they could, printing headlines such as "Ex-flame Burns Ex-lover" when a former girlfriend testified against a defendant.

My team and I became well-known in the small town. The deli/ice cream store named a sundae after one of my colleagues, and I was recognized as the lawyer when shopping at the mall or running errands. It was an interesting glimpse into small, or at least smaller, hometown life.

No one patronized me in my wheelchair. If people had questions or concerns about it, they openly asked. We stayed at a large local hotel called The Five Seasons, where the staff treated us like family. Some of them even invited us into their homes for the Thanksgiving holiday. They treated us like celebrities and always wanted to know the latest thing happening in the trial. The hotel was surprisingly accessible for 1989 (pre-ADA), and it was close to the courthouse and unfortunately, noisy train tracks.

Toward the end of the trial, one of the defense attorneys suggested I had misrepresented evidence to the court. This was fighting talk. Such suggestions implied I was a liar. The gloves were off.

The next day, before court began, he approached me in the courthouse lobby and pointed to his hair.

"Do you see this haircut?" he said.

"Yes," I mumbled, confused about his point. But his hair was certainly a bit askew.

"This is what happens to persons in this town who insult the prosecutor," he said. "I insulted you yesterday, and I apologize."

"Thanks," I said. "However, you made your comments in public, so you can make your apology in public, too."

He was surprised and took a step back. Then he looked at me for a minute, and with a half-smile, nodded. He made the apology his first point when the court resumed, and he never underestimated me again. Mutual respect had been gained. I was learning to use my voice on my behalf, not just for others.

All three of the defendants were found guilty. A sentencing date was set, and they were sent to jail to await their reckoning.

After my success at the Iowa trial, I was rewarded with my next case. It involved seven trips in one year to Hawaii, as well as one trip to Lima, Peru. Such a hard life for a travel addict.

On the first trip to Hawaii, several colleagues accompanied me. They were each assigned to exquisite top-floor rooms with balconies and an ocean view. My second-floor room, on the other hand, was in a tower at the rear of the property, with a view of the hotel's neon sign located directly over the open-air karaoke bar. It was nonstop noise every night, with visiting tourists croaking along out of tune to "My Way" and "New York, New York," among others. What they lacked in quality, they compensated for in volume.

Soon, I learned the hotel's policy was to put people labeled "handicapped" on this floor. To them, it was convenient, as all the handicapped-accessible requirements could be limited to one location. However, to me, it suggested that the most vulnerable hotel guests could be easy targets, and everyone would know where to find an easy victim.

Upon returning to D.C., I wrote a letter to the hotel about this situation. I was impressed to receive a phone call from a concerned manager. He ended his call by inviting me to call his office for our reservations on our next trip. Naturally, I did.

The next time we visited, we were given rooms in a special wing with a pool, seating area, and ocean balcony. A large basket of goodies and some celebratory adult beverages arrived in my room.

At the end of our week there, I went with some of my colleagues to personally thank the manager for his attention. I asked him if I could continue making my reservations through his office. He responded in the affirmative, but I thought I detected a slight wince a moment later when he realized what he had agreed to. My colleagues and I enjoyed the same excellent accommodation on our subsequent trips.

WIDE HORIZONS

Following some jockeying with employees and supervisors at the Justice Department, my job no longer felt like a comfortable fit for me. I was ready for a new challenge, so I accepted an offer to move over to the Treasury Department as the chief of the International Section, dealing with financial crimes. The office worked with the Justice Department on an international level to convince countries to adopt procedures and regulations to inhibit money laundering. The job involved a lot of, wait for it, travel, especially to South America.

My first foray overseas was with a small delegation to Peru, Bolivia, and Columbia. In 1993, airlines were not equipped for people in wheelchairs. There were no air bridges linking the terminal to the plane. One of my colleagues, Carlos, gallantly became my ticket to accessibility. He boldly carried me up and down the mobile stairway brought to the plane. Eventually, we worked out how best to do this, but I took my shoes off before he lifted me. They had a habit of falling off when I was being carried. My colleague and I reached the top of the steps, and inevitably, a flight attendant said something like, "Aww, honeymooners." On one occasion, the entire plane broke into applause, and we were feted with champagne.

In Bolivia, representatives from the U.S. Embassy met us at the gate and gave us aspirin to take as we were arriving at the airport with one of the highest altitudes in the world. After carrying me down the stairway, Carlos was decidedly breathless.

Frequently, in hotels, I couldn't squeeze the chair through the bathroom doorway, or navigate the bathtub. However, most tubs included handheld showers which I could use. Needless to say, many bathroom floors suffered a good soaking.

On one trip returning from Bolivia, a huge protest blocked the road to the airport. Unable to pass through it, we missed our flight. We returned to the embassy to reschedule the flight and found that the only alternative route included an overnight stay in Panama.

We arrived in Panama in the early morning hours. My colleagues were exhausted, and everyone went straight to their Marriott Hotel rooms. When I entered mine, the bathroom door was too narrow. I called the desk, and they sent up a manager. They had me check out several rooms. They were all the same, and finally, the manager conceded his hotel was not wheelchair accessible. So, at three in the morning in a dark city, they sent me by taxi to another hotel. I had no idea where it was or where to tell my colleagues to find me, but at last, I had a bathroom and a bed. The next morning, I simply waited to be found by my colleagues. (We had no cell phones in the 1990s.) Fortunately, they did find me.

Several years later, we were scheduled to return to Panama. We had reservations at the same high-rise Marriott Hotel unable to accommodate me on the previous visit. My Spanish-speaking colleague, Carlos, called ahead and explained what had happened on our last visit. He questioned whether they had made any changes to make the hotel accessible and was assured they had.

We arrived in Panama and checked in, only to find the room was no different than before. The bathroom was still totally inaccessible. We cornered the manager, gave him the history, and explained the problem. The hotel arranged for me to stay in a suite for one night, where I could reach some of the facilities. The next night, they gave me a room where they had destroyed the wall to the bathroom to make enough room for the wheelchair to enter. They rewarded my patience with a delicious dessert left on a side table, with an apology note for the inconvenience.

The next morning, at the elevator bank, I saw another woman in a wheelchair. I went straight to the manager to ask how they were going to accommodate her. "Don't worry, Ms. Broderick," the manager said. "We've knocked down a wall for her, too."

While at the Treasury Department, I went with a team to a conference in Kuala Lumpur, Malaysia, to train on money laundering initiatives. I was accompanied by office colleagues as well as Customs Department agents. The conference went well, leaving us with some free time to see the sights. We toured a pewter factory, explored the city, and visited Batu Caves. Legend has it that if a single woman walks up and down the enormous staircase leading to the caves, she will become pregnant within a year. I felt some relief, knowing it was unlikely to apply to me. My colleagues wanted to explore the caves but felt guilty about leaving me alone. One of the burly customs agents tossed me onto his back, piggyback style, so we all completed the tour together. Once again, we had to be careful with my shoes. Tiny monkeys scampered around, grabbing anything they could. I am happy to report that no single monkey was injured during this jaunt, but I did see the customs guy rubbing his back afterward.

Eventually, I was loaned back to the Justice Department to work on a new initiative to address violence against women. The Violence Against Women Act, supported by Senator Joe Biden, had recently been passed. A new office was created at the Justice Department to support the act, and the newly appointed head of the office was Bonnie Campbell, a tall redhead who hailed from Iowa. (While I had been trying my case in Iowa, Ms. Campbell was the state's attorney general.) So, although we had never previously met, we knew of each other. Bonnie welcomed me to her office with open arms. Our work there was on the front lines of the women's movement when domestic violence issues were finally being recognized. We worked closely with the White House and its staff to support, implement, and promote the Violence Against Women Act. We provided support information and organized events and proclamations. We harvested our data by speaking with survivors of violence. There were so many sad women's faces and tragic case histories. I can't recall any details, just how massive a challenge we faced.

I had stayed in touch with Judge Harry Greene since my clerkship, frequently visiting him when prosecuting cases in the courthouse and seeking his advice on career choices. While I was at the U.S. Attorney's Office, he once asked me when I was going to apply to be a judge. I was surprised. I had not been practicing law for long and was shocked he knew someday I wanted to be a judge. But I felt too inexperienced and had told him so.

But Harry refused to let go of his question, "When are you going to apply?"

Finally, I decided if I applied, his prodding ought to cease.

My name came up for consideration before the United States Senate while I was working with the savvy and smart Bonnie Campbell at the Department of Justice. I could never have foreseen how fortunate my relationship with her would turn out to be.

CHAPTER

17

ADA STARTS TO BITE

Some three years after the ADA had passed Congress and became Law, it was still obvious to me that on the street, it would take a lot longer to change long-entrenched discriminatory attitudes and working practices. Parking facilities were slowly beginning to incorporate special bays spacious enough for loading and unloading wheelchairs. Guide and service dogs were more readily accepted on public transport. Communications devices were being adapted and ramps were appearing on pavements but not everywhere.

I had an opportunity to make an enduring impression at the Treasury Department, and it had nothing to do with money laundering. The office building was an imposing and aging edifice located directly to the east of the White House, separated by a pedestrian-only street. Employees used the main entrance on Fifteenth Street, which was not wheelchair accessible. People with a mobility impairment were obliged to use the door designated for packages and deliveries, thirty feet north of the main entrance. After ringing the bell, they had to wait for one of the federal agents inside to unlock it. There was no shelter from the weather, and often, the delay was long. I jokingly referred to the delivery entrance as my "separate but equal" door.

I usually tried to avoid it by using the basement entrance, which also presented challenges. Its colloquial name, "the moat," was fitting. Access required rolling down a long, steep, cobblestone driveway at the side of the building — an intimidating journey. Smokers took their breaks at this doorway, so users of the basement entrance often had to run a smoky gauntlet to access the workplace.

One day, I ate my lunch outside the building and decided to take the separate but equal door back inside. As I approached, I saw some workers clustered at the main entrance and wondered what was going on. Once inside, I went over and saw tripods bearing signs announcing a new entrance with artists' impressions showing what it was to look like. I peered at it carefully but did not see anything in the graphics remotely resembling a ramp.

I went directly to the office of the building engineer and asked to see the head guy. He listened graciously as I explained the drawings for the new entrance didn't include a ramp for the mobility-impaired.

"Because there is no ramp," he said.

"But surely, there has to be a ramp," I said.

"It's not required," he said.

"Under the Americans with Disabilities Act, it is now required," I said.

"It's a historic building," he said. "The rules don't apply."

"Ordinarily, that might be true," I said. "But if the historic property is renovated, access must be provided under the ADA."

"I don't think so," he said, dismissing me with a wave of the hand.

"I need to tell you it is my understanding," I said, smiling sweetly. "I should also inform you I plan to quit my position at the Treasury Department shortly, and it won't bother me one iota to file a lawsuit as my parting gift."

He stopped smiling.

After a pause, he picked up the phone and asked for the building architect. The architect confirmed the need for a ramp and began to revise the plans immediately.

Every time I go by the Fifteenth Street entrance, I look at the ramp and smile. It doesn't bear my name but those who know me are familiar with its origins.

Occasionally, the treasury undersecretary stopped by to say hello to staff. At my cubicle, he sat for a while in the rolling desk chair allocated to me but surplus to requirements. It remained for visitors. After several minutes of wriggling about, he declared the chair was exceedingly comfortable, unlike the one in his office. I suggested he take it. This led to further discussion, and he decided to take the chair. However, there was one condition.

He whispered it to me.

I agreed with pleasure.

We went together to the main hallway, an impressive central area with floor tiles alternating in black and white marble squares. I was in my chair; he scooted along in his. We rolled down to his floor, out of the elevator, and lined up, side by side, in the hallway, facing toward his office in the far corner. The undersecretary began the countdown, and then we were off. It was a race to the finish. The result remains classified to this day.

My direct supervisor was horrified. "How unprofessional," he exclaimed. What he meant was: "No woman on his watch, never mind one in a wheelchair, was going to pal around with the undersecretary. It was a spot reserved for him."

My relationship with this petty-minded man rapidly soured. He found numerous ways to make my work life miserable and resorted to skewering me in public meetings. It was clear I was bumping my head against a glass ceiling with no wheelchair-friendly escape route to be found. My position had become untenable. It was time to move a step closer to my dream. I would become a judge.

CHAPTER

18

THE LONG WAIT

Each state and jurisdiction has its own procedures for filling judicial vacancies. Federal judge positions are the most enviable, as they are lifetime positions. However, they are not easy to come by, and need popular recognition in the field of law, professional support, and political contacts to even start to be noticed. Most state judges are elected. Some are in a contested two-way election, while others are appointed by the governor and run, usually unopposed, and retained after subsequent elections.

As a federal city, D.C. is unique. Applicants must be D.C. residents with appropriate legal experience. Each candidate had to complete a lengthy and hugely daunting application form. Once submitted, each new applicant was granted a fifteen-minute interview before the Judicial Nomination Committee, which then selected three applicants for each vacancy. Those three names were sent to the White House Counsel's Office for more interviews.

One of the three would be recommended to the President of the United States, who made the final call. The chosen nominee then had to be confirmed by the Senate's Governmental Affairs Committee.

According to advice received for writing résumés, I knew I should honestly but bravely describe how my former employers would have died without my valuable contributions. This was not a problem for most lawyers, who normally brimmed with self-confidence, but not me. My qualifications were extensive, including varied trial experience and appropriate judicial temperament. The application required me to address every aspect of my life and pinpoint several cases I considered significant. I had to explain why they were significant and what I learned from them.

I wrote about some of my hard criminal cases and what I had gleaned from trying them, meeting witnesses, and talking to jurors. I was required to provide contact information for my opposing lawyers in those cases. Because my level of confidence was low and I didn't think I had enough experience to have a real chance to get the job anyway, I took my time and didn't get overly stressed about it. Still, it was a huge relief when I finally finished the application. The completed document was thirty-seven pages. Then came my fifteen-minute interview with the Judicial Nomination Commission.

The committee was made up of representatives from local courts, city government, and the White House. I had just fifteen minutes to convince them to select me to be put forward for approval by the White House counsel.

I didn't make the cut.

And was not informed why.

Thankfully, applicants who were not offered a position had their applications retained. Thereafter, they were contacted each time a new vacancy occurred at the court, and they could indicate whether they were still interested in the position.

After two or three years of rejections, I did not hold out much hope. However, after talking to some colleagues, I eventually learned why I failed to make progress. In my naïveté, I assumed I just had to apply and attend the interview, whereas what I needed to do was build a public profile by networking. The concept was alien to me. I believe suitability for any position should be measured on ability, not on who you know. A typical female mistake.

When discussing this with other applicants, I discovered that their references had personally contacted the committee members to lobby on their behalf. I called up a dear friend who had contacts everywhere and told her I was going to ask for a favor. I told her I hated using a friend in this way, but I needed someone well-connected. To cut a long story short, I asked her to be my campaign manager.

"Of course I will," she said. "What are friends for?"

Things began to happen almost immediately.

She introduced me to people who advised me how to beef up my application, press for a second interview, and prepare for the questions. Before I knew it, strangers were contacting me for telephone interviews and reporting back to people who could reach members of the commission. I was learning what networking could do.

I was excited to be invited to a second interview. It was going well, and then one of the interviewers said, "I hear you ski. Did you know the blind judge skis, too?"

Hmmm, I thought. *I bet half the judges on the bench ski, but I am only compared with the blind judge.* I realized then they did not yet see me in the same light as other applicants and were unlikely to alter their entrenched mindsets to accommodate me. This was going to be a long haul.

I discussed this with my campaign manager and others who supported me. We decided to explain to the members of the committee that a wheelchair was no hindrance to judging. One of my contacts spoke directly with the head of the committee. Amazingly, once they heard from my friend that all she needed was a ramp for the bench, they were delighted. When the next vacancy opened, my name went to the White House for nomination.

I'd navigated one barrier — one of many.

D.C. judges are a special breed. Although we hear local cases, we are federal judges since D.C. is not a state and does not have state judges. As I mentioned earlier, after the committee selects three candidates for each vacancy, their names go to the White House. In this case, President Bill Clinton officially named the final nominee, to be then approved by the U.S. Congress. However, candidates do not go before the Judiciary Committee in the manner of most federal judges. Instead, they are approved by the Governmental Affairs Committee, which oversees matters concerning the District of Columbia. If they pass, the Senate must give a final, full vote.

I was rolling down the hallway at the Justice Department when an official told me — in confidence — that I had been selected as the White House's nominee for the judicial position. He told me to act surprised when I received the official notification phone call from the White House, which occurred a short time later. For the remainder of the day, there was a flurry of messages and calls. I was excited, ecstatic, and on cloud nine. But, had no idea how tough the next two years would be — or what falling off a cloud might feel like.

Toward the end of the Senate session, senators were already heading home for the Christmas holidays. A new post-election Senate began in the new year, and my nomination had to be re-sent to them. The delays had begun.

The first was from the committee accepting the nomination. They requested I complete an additional thirty-seven-page application explaining it was a new application with different questions. I read it through carefully, as judges do, but didn't see one single new question. A June hearing date was set, only to be canceled the week before. Rumors started: There was a problem with my nomination.

My colleagues had previously said, "You will sail through. Who will reject a woman in a wheelchair?" But now, I finally achieved the equality for which I was striving. There was no free judge pass for the mobility-impaired. I was being treated as poorly as all applicants.

Newspapers started publishing ugly articles about me. Radio broadcasts included unflattering stories containing rumors, innuendos, and untruths. I was accused of being bitter, handicapped, and anti-Hispanic. Someone was trying to paint me as a heartless, biased prosecutor. But who and why?

These are familiar laments from public figures nowadays, but this had never happened to me. Where had all the vitriol come from? Who felt so threatened by a woman in a wheelchair they needed to resort to such underhanded tactics? I will never know for sure, but rumor has it this was political strife between a senator and an attorney at the White House who happened to use a wheelchair. When I was nominated, someone falsely assumed this White House attorney and I were good friends because we were both in wheelchairs. This hint of potential collusion between the mobility-impaired had piqued the senator's ire. He was adamant no friends of White House staff would be confirmed under his watch.

A reporter from a legal publication phoned me for comments about the ugly things being said in the news. I declined as politely as I could, given my enraged state of mind. (Was this to be typical of life as a judge? I'd hoped for support, not derogatory comments with no basis of truth.) Bonnie Campbell had offered me a quote to use at moments like this: "Never pick a fight with someone who buys their ink by the barrel." I also applied Judge Millsap's sage advice from long ago: "Just take a big gulp."

I asked the reporter why her publication hadn't interviewed anyone who took my side. She asked me to suggest names of people she could contact, which I provided. She called back later in the day to tell me she hadn't been able to reach any of my contacts and was leaving for the weekend. Her story, unchanged, was to be published on Monday. So much for balanced reporting.

I wondered whether someone in the corridors of power felt so desperately insecure that they were vehemently opposed to the idea of a female judge, even more so against one in a wheelchair. It felt humiliating to have my hard-won reputation and character attacked with no way to fight back. I realized any attempt I made to refute the allegations sounded gratuitous and defensive, so I resorted to tried-and-tested tactics.

I put on a confident front and attended public events and professional get-togethers. I wore my best suit and lots of jewelry and smiled from ear to ear. Sometimes, you just have to be your own press corps.

Finally, the White House counsel called to inform me about a problem in my FBI report, one of the background investigations carried out on all nominees. The report was confidential, however, so the counsel couldn't tell the problem.

One day at the office, I was talking to Bonnie Campbell about the latest developments. I was frustrated and upset as I watched my dreams being yanked away from me. I didn't know why it was happening or what to do about it. Bonnie heard and shared my frustration. She called her friend, Senator Tom Harkin of Iowa, to see if he could help. She asked me to write a memo explaining the situation to him. I was working in my office a brief time later when Bonnie called.

"Come on down to my office," she said. "We're going to see Senator Harkin."

We drove to the Senate Office Building, where we were welcomed in the senator's reception area and escorted into his private office. After a polite welcome and introduction, the senator excused all his other staff members, closed his office door, and sat down to chat with me.

I had never been in a senator's office, nor had I spoken personally with one. I was in awe. The room was huge, with a ceiling that seemed to go up to the sky. There was a desk, but the office was set up like a living room. The senator sat beside me and began by explaining he had seen the FBI report about me. He said he could not tell me what was in the report, but he could ask me questions based on what he had read. His questions began. An hour later, the senator asked me, "Pat, what do you think is going on here?"

"I don't know, Senator," I replied.

Again, he asked me, "Pat, what do you think is going on here?"

"I don't know, Senator," I replied a second time.

"Pat." He paused. "What do you think is going on here?"

I took a deep breath and said, "Senator, I'm unsure. But I do know people generally want to help me until I want the same things they do. Then things turn ugly."

"That's it," he shouted as he stood up. "I've seen this with my brother, who is deaf, and my nephew, who is a quadriplegic. You're supposed to stay quiet and be grateful."

He called Bonnie back into the room and then said to me, "Don't ever give up without calling me first. I will see what I can do."

A few weeks later, I received another call from the White House. The Senate Committee had informed them they intended to reject my nomination and return it to the White House.

I phoned Senator Harkin's office immediately and explained what I had been told. The senator called me, listened carefully to what had happened, and said he would get back in touch. He was true to his word. Later the same Friday night, he called and told me to come to the Senate Office to meet with one of the senators on the Governmental Affairs Committee at ten o'clock the next morning.

I met with the Government Affairs Committee Senator Carl Levin and his administrative assistant for about an hour and a half on a Saturday morning in a nearly empty building echoing with passing footsteps. The senator, who was short and balding, with a friendly face, had been a defense attorney. As such, he might have held a bias against a former prosecutor. His assistant, a professional woman a bit younger than I, observed me intensely. She seemed to take everything in, including my mood, body language, and words.

The assistant occasionally translated for the senator. I sensed he assumed the nasty things written about me were true. But he gave me his focused attention, grilled me, listened to his assistant, and seemed genuinely and pleasantly surprised by my responses. He didn't leave any clue if my nomination was going to be approved, though.

Before any official hearing in front of the Governmental Affairs Committee, two senators on the committee were to have their staff interview me. The first senator's staff asked whether I was bringing my wheelchair-bound friends in to protest during the committee hearing. They continued in this vein to ask questions with no legal relevance. The second group of staffers acted tough. One said, "We hear you are extremely aggressive as a prosecutor. You're often in the witness's face, yelling and screaming at them."

"As a prosecutor," I said, "I consider myself assertive rather than aggressive. Men are praised for being aggressive. But when women are assertive, they are frequently called aggressive — and other names beginning with a *b* containing five letters."

The female staffer chuckled as one of the men counted letters on his fingers. "I must add," I said, "I cannot yell. I am physically paralyzed from the chest down and cannot access the muscles required for a good yell or scream. Finally, I must point out that the witness box is at least one step, if not more, up from my floor level. There is no way I can physically reach the face of any witness."

By the looks on their faces, I had made progress.

My hearing date was finally scheduled — to occur on the anniversary of my paralyzing car accident. *It will be a grand day for me to receive my wings and soar*, I thought.

On the day of the hearing, I drove to the Senate Office Building on Capitol Hill with plenty of time to spare. I parked, extracted my wheelchair, and went through security to the hearing room where, of course, there was no wheelchair-accessible bathroom adjacent. But I did spot masses of space available for my coachloads of imaginary wheelchair buddies as they rolled in to the lobby for my appointment.

Three judicial nominees were heard at this hearing. The questioning for the first two was polite and genial. And then it was my turn.

One senator asked a question. It was so long, so clearly biased, and so obviously meant to put me on the defensive that I wondered if the staffers had been up all night composing it. But this was the anniversary of my accident, the day I reminded myself to survive one more year. And I intended to survive and thrive. I ignored the senator's question but thanked him for asking it and then told the committee what they needed to hear.

I endured three further questions, each one blatantly digging for dirt in my three worst jury trials. Every prosecutor has bad trials. These three were later referred to the court of appeals and reversed. The senators used this information to discredit me.

I didn't let them get away with it. When I finished answering the last question, I looked at the senator and said, "Sir, during my career, I've handled hundreds of cases and taken over seventy to trial. You have asked me about only three of those. What about the other successful ones? I've always done my best to be fair and just. I never said I was perfect, but I am proud of my record. Any prosecutor would be."

As the hearing ended, the senators came down and shook my hand. One of them said, "Those were hard questions, and your answers were fine."

At last, I was making progress, but had I cleared the final fence? Was my nomination going to be confirmed? I'd have to wait and see.

YOUR HONOR

During the waiting period between my nomination and confirmation, it was important not to appear overconfident or anxious. Rumor had it that one nominee had gone to the judge's chambers and began taking measurements for his new furniture. He was never confirmed. I had no idea how long the Senate was going to take to decide. The waiting proved tedious and nerve-wracking.

It's strange waiting. No one knows when or if you might be leaving your job to become a judge. In private practice, a long wait can be monetarily difficult. Your colleagues congratulate you on your nomination, but they then demand the return of files before showing you the door. As a federal worker, I was fortunate to remain employed, but I never knew how long the Senate might take to act on my case.

During this time, I was part of a mentorship program at my law school. I had randomly been assigned a mentee, and a cocktail party was scheduled so mentors and mentees could become acquainted. I liked Marcie, my mentee, immediately. She was a bubbly young woman of Italian heritage with long raven hair. I thought she was genuine, full of laughter and fun. I was delighted to make her acquaintance and felt confident we would get along.

I invited her to be my first law clerk. She happily accepted. There was just one tiny problem. I was still waiting for my appointment to be confirmed.

As a Superior Court judge, I was entitled to two full-time staff members: a secretary, later retitled to a judicial administrative assistant (JAA), and a judicial law clerk. Law clerks were traditionally new law school graduates who had not yet passed the bar exam. For them, it is a year of training and learning how the court and judges work and an opportunity to build a network of well-placed contacts. For those interested in litigation or appellate work, it can be considered a prestigious position, depending on the level of court they work in.

The long road to my confirmation dragged on and on. Marcie had completed her law degree long before she became my law clerk, but she cheerfully took on doc review while we waited for the Senate to make up their mind. Doc review is a temporary and tedious job reviewing documents for large firms; it's the dreaded standby for out-of-work lawyers.

Then, out of nowhere, it happened.

On the last day of the Senate's fall session of 1998, my appointment was confirmed. I was sworn in as an associate judge of the Superior Court of the District of Columbia the very next day.

After patiently waiting, the call to attend my investiture came with about an hour's notice. I lived nearby, but Marcie had one hour to drag herself off the sofa at home in Annapolis, get ready, and drive into D.C. The chief judge wanted to do an informal swearing-in immediately.

It had taken six years from my initial application, and two years, thirty-one days since my original nomination. (But, hey, who was counting?) It was an extraordinary waiting time, one of the longest in the court's history. But finally, Judge Broderick had arrived.

During the two years of waiting, I had requested, under the Freedom of Information Act, a copy of my supposedly disastrous FBI report. About eighteen months after my investiture, it arrived, fully redacted. In other words, anyone who wished to be anonymous was permitted to remain anonymous. Any information the FBI requested to keep private had been crossed out. Consequently, all I saw were a lot of black lines.

During the lengthy confirmation process, the court figured out they needed to install a wheelchair lift in at least one of the courtrooms. It was the first one ever in a courtroom. They also prepared the chambers closest to the courtroom to be handicapped accessible. They painted a handicapped sign on one of the parking spots in the court's garage. This was the first handicapped parking space ever in D.C. Superior Court, eight years after the ADA had passed. I was thrilled by these changes, even if many of my new colleagues were not. They wanted to know why the new judge had been assigned a courtroom with chambers adjacent when they had not.

A few years later, I was appointed to the coveted Felony One calendar while still a new judge. Resentment seethed again. Felony One handles homicides and serious sexual assaults. It is extremely challenging, both at the level of lawyering and the pressures of high-profile work. According to some of my fellow judges, I received favored treatment *because* of my disability. Some thought I used my disability to land plum assignments. I realized as a mobility-impaired person, I am not expected to be an achiever seeking equality. Credit for *ability* is rarely given to those who have a disability.

IN THE COURTROOM

Everything in my life had prepared me well for what I was about to hear and observe from behind the judge's bench.

I was once a normal, whole, walking person who loved to dance. My accident, recovery, and life in a wheelchair introduced me to unique emotions and experiences almost unheard of in the aloof world of judges.

As I age, my body degenerates, but my brain still thinks and feels pretty much as it always has. My creaky bits and an increasing number of wrinkles remind me time is slipping by. In this respect, I am no different from anyone else, except I can't sense creaks anywhere other than my arms and shoulders.

I am extremely familiar with what it's like to be instantly judged and pigeonholed because of my appearance. Because I am mobility-impaired, the skills or wisdom I have to offer are often disregarded — even though I am as educated and experienced as a normal person. I don't see myself as handicapped. I see myself as a regular person who happens to use a wheelchair rather than a set of legs to get around. I call it "differently abled" or "mobility-impaired." There are many discussions these days about the correct terminology to describe folks like me. Certainly, words such as crippled and invalid are currently taboo, and handicapped and disabled are on their way out, too.

At first, I didn't care what words were used to describe me. But now I have a better sense of the power of language. I tell people it begins with a *person*: a person with a disability, a person with a mobility impairment, or a person with a physical handicap. Try to remember to acknowledge our shared humanity.

I have come to understand fear can be a frequent companion. This includes fear of the future, fear of failure, fear of the unknown, and sometimes the fear of success.

I understand what it is like to be treated as a non-person, as a thing to be reluctantly dealt with, a non-entity of little or no importance, who is not worthy of being understood. There is a fear of being ignored or unacknowledged. How long will I be dead before someone notices? I have learned how to fight fear daily; I know how to win or lose the battle with fear. This is something unique I bring to my work.

Frequently, people think they are helping me when they are not. They don't empathize or listen to what I might need. They assume the help they have decided to give me is valid and welcome. Yet they make me feel like a bulky object to be transported, like a refrigerator or their latest charity, when all I want to do is to show up under my own steam and be treated like everyone else. My Australian mom sometimes described a person as "cold as charity." While I understand well-meaning strangers are just trying to be kind, my resulting loss of dignity can sometimes smolder long and deep. The pain of not being heard or listened to lingers. Some people are simply incapable of understanding the world through my eyes or even looking into those eyes.

I have also been treated with tremendous sensitivity and kindness.

I might not bring a set of working legs to the bench, but my experiences as a differently abled person have served me well. They give me a unique and wider perspective and add value to any set of circumstances I encounter. I am not looking for praise. I'm just hoping people understand that different can be beautiful, helpful, and uniquely good.

When I started work on the judge's bench, I received two court assignments. One was Family Motions; the other was Mental Health.

In the Family Motions assignment, the Office of the Attorney General (OAG) brought cases against people who were not paying child support and whose former partners were receiving federal assistance.

The court listened to the evidence and made a ruling. If the court found the person did have the ability and means to make a financial contribution but had failed to do so, a fine could be imposed, and the defendant could be found in contempt of a court order.

There was a presumption unless proven otherwise, anyone could come up with at least fifty dollars a month. Most of the defendants were not represented by lawyers and readily said they were not paying for child support. Some admitted even while unemployed they still found the means to buy their weekly ration of marijuana — this was not a particularly good defense position. Some said they couldn't work because of an injury, often a knee injury while playing basketball or football. One gentleman told me he was a boxing coach but had hurt his leg, so he couldn't coach.

"Can't you coach while sitting down?" I asked.

His face took on a deer-in-the-headlights expression, and he couldn't fabricate any response.

If the court made a finding there was an acceptance of parentage, sufficient financial means, and a current court order, the defendant should have been paying child support. It could order the defendant to be jailed until the amount the court ordered had been paid. It was called criminal contempt. The contempt could be cured by paying up either the money owed or a different amount specified by the court. After making that determination, I always let the defendants make their first call from the courtroom clerk's phone. There were no cell phones in wide use then. Inevitably, they called their current girlfriend to ask for financial support.

"Which case is this one?" said one male defendant.

"How many cases do you have?" I asked.

"Oh, three others," he said, each one with a different woman.

He asked to speak with his newest lady out in the hallway. She was number five, he said, and would bail him out. And she did.

On a cold and bitter February day, a disheveled-looking white man of around forty with stringy, greasy hair stood before me. He was accompanied by a boy about two years old who was wearing nothing but shorts and a tee shirt.

"Can you tell me how you propose to pay the maintenance for your wife and children?" I asked.

"I've left them to pursue my music, and I now have a new family," he said, gesturing to the boy. Indeed, he had left a secure, well-paid position to follow his musical ambitions and start a second family. "I'll pay the child support to my first family when I can, but after I take care of my current family."

"Your timeline is not acceptable," I said. "You pay up or go to jail. Your first family needs to eat now, not when you are ready to pay."

"No," he said. "You can't put me in jail. I have my son with me."

"No problem," I said. "Social Services will take care of your child."

"No," he yelled as the U.S. Marshals approached to detain him. He snatched his child and stomped toward the bench. The marshals whisked me out of danger, and the spectators emptied the courtroom in a grand rush. The courtroom was frozen in a stand-off, with the defendant holding onto his child and the marshals trying to coax him to put the child down and go with them. He finally put the child down, and a Social Services worker remained with the child. A brief time later, after the courtroom deputy placed a call, the new partner arrived to rescue her child, at which time, with a look of disgust, she paid the defendant's fine and left. I wondered how much longer their relationship might survive.

On the Mental Health calendar, petitions were presented to the court requesting someone to be admitted involuntarily to the local mental hospital, St. Elizabeth's. A request had to be accompanied by a doctor's statement confirming the patient was mentally ill and a danger to themselves or others. Once such a request was granted, the patient was hospitalized but given a court hearing within twenty-four hours. The affidavits and hearings proved interesting.

Because of the location of the court, several cases involved people who had attempted to enter the White House. One lady had driven up to the gate and asked the guard to grant her admission into her office. The guard had no information permitting her entrance. While speaking with her through her car window, he spotted a loose round of ammunition on her dashboard. She was immediately arrested by the Secret Service, who impounded her vehicle. Inside, along with the unexpended bullet, they found a dinner knife and a wig. The Secret Service decided that she was armed and dangerous and might have intended to use the wig as a disguise.

At her trial, she admitted she possessed the knife because she frequently ate in the car or used it to deter curious gentlemen who approached her vehicle. She used a wig because she was a woman of mature years who liked to look nice and could not afford a hairdresser. Sadly, she remained convinced the President had called her and offered her a top job in his office.

Another woman, beautifully manicured and with wild hair, threw an object over the White House gate. It turned out to be lipstick and a makeup case. When questioned by the Secret Service, she advised President Clinton was waiting for her and that they were in love. A subsequent search of her apartment revealed a dedicated room decorated with photos, magazine articles, and several TV sets looping various tapes, all with the President as the subject.

After a fire in his apartment, a gentleman charged with arson was crystal clear with his justification: "Of course, I have all my appliances switched on permanently. Who wouldn't? I only live nine miles from the CIA building and have many windows pointing in their direction. Everyone understands the only way to protect oneself is to jam the airwaves with one's electrical appliances."

In another criminal case, I was taking a guilty plea from a woman in her thirties. She had large, expressive eyes and appeared to be listening intently to my questions. We were almost through the plea colloquy when I asked the standard question, "Has anybody threatened you or forced you to plead guilty?"

There was a long pause.

Then she looked up at me with widened eyes and exclaimed, "If you mean the satellite on the roof, then yes."

It was the end of her plea agreement.

We scheduled her for a forensic exam with a psychologist to assess whether she was mentally competent to make legal decisions and follow court procedures.

If anything was surprising about these cases, it was the amount of fear, pain, and loneliness people experienced and the different ways they found to cope. Having been through a major life transition myself, I respected the unique efforts of my fellow citizens to survive — even if it was in their alternate world. I was concerned about their loneliness and the lack of family, friends, and resources available to them. I don't recall any one of them ever having a family member show up in court on their behalf. It humbled me.

Because of revised court staffing needs, I remained on those calendars for only a few months, and then I switched to the Neglect caseload, which was referred to as the Family Division in those days.

One heartbreaking case I'll never forget involved a young girl, around four years old, who was living in a foster home with another young boy of similar age. They had both been removed from their respective homes because of neglect by their biological parents.

The proceedings for the day were over, and the courtroom had emptied except for the children and their foster mother. They began to relax and chat.

I asked the young girl if she wanted to sit in the witness box. She jumped right up, scampered over, and sat right down. Then, with a grin, she pulled the microphone toward her and began singing, "You are my sunshine, my only sunshine." The boy jumped up, went to the front of the witness box, leaned in toward his foster sister, and sang along with her, "You make me happy when skies are gray." The children grinned at one another with pure, simple joy. It was clear, at least for the moment, they were safe, cared for, and happy.

Another case came before me, where the parents had allegedly neglected their three children, ages five, two-and-a-half, and eight months. The oldest child confidently answered questions during the proceedings. It transpired his parents left him in charge when they went out. He said he was happy to care for his siblings and demonstrated how he fed the infant by heating her milk and then testing the temperature on his arm. When asked what he did when his toddler sister cried, he explained, "I either hug her or give her one of my toys."

His parents simply did not understand why three children under six years old could not be left for hours on their own. After hearing from both the parents and the child, it was clear who the more mature party was.

I keep a bowl of sweets, usually chocolate kisses, in my chambers to present a welcoming ambiance. After the hearing, I asked the boy if he wanted some.

He replied, "Yes, please."

I nodded toward the bowl.

He took one chocolate.

"Is that all you want?" I asked.

"Yes," he replied. Then, after a moment's hesitation, he added, "Can I take some for my sisters?"

"Of course," I said.

He returned to the dish, grabbed a fistful, and stuffed his pocket so full he spilled a trail of chocolate kisses as he went out the door.

Some of these children's living conditions were dire. Social workers often presented pictures when giving evidence, sometimes showing homes bereft of anything but a blanket on the floor, trash, and occasionally rats. Many of the parents were frequently absent and had no idea of their responsibilities. Most had grown up in similar environments, without role models or mentors to guide them.

Despite their history of neglect, somehow the children seemed capable of retaining joy and perspective. I found it fulfilling to watch how they gradually improved after being placed in a more caring environment.

One young girl placed with a foster family began to develop discipline problems as she entered her teens, possibly because she was unaccustomed to house rules or asking permission before doing things. She was desperate to have her ears pierced. Her foster mother refused unless permission was granted by the court. Without court permission, the foster mother could have been sued by the birth parents or the state. The foster mother happily applied to the court, and they appeared before me.

I was thrilled to hear the girl whining about holes in her ears, as it demonstrated she was making some progress away from her wild, undisciplined upbringing and was adapting to a more normal family life and perspective. I granted permission for her to get her ears pierced, and she was ecstatic. I asked her if she wanted to sit in the witness box, and she did, followed by the judge's bench. As she stood beside the microphone, I asked her, remembering all the horror and poor conditions she had been through, what she might have ordered if she were a judge and could order anything.

She thought for a moment and then leaned into the microphone and said, "A McDonald's hamburger."

A young boy came before me in a neglect case. His parents were found to have been neglectful toward the boy. The government was seeking to take the child from his parents for his safety. The child was represented by an attorney. His parents had an attorney. The government had an attorney. Furthermore, the child had a guardian *ad litem* who was yet another attorney. Unlike the attorney representing the child, whose job was to win the case for his client, the job of the guardian *ad litem* was to independently decide what was in the best interests of the child and to advocate for that.

Before the proceedings began, and when the lawyers haggled in the courtroom, the guardian *ad litem* became unhappy with the government's position. When the government declined to agree with him, he began harassing their female attorney.

The guardian was a large Caucasian man with long hair spilling over his broad shoulders. When he hovered over the government lawyer, he was quite imposing. He pursued her around the courtroom, haranguing her to agree with him. He also threatened to refer her for unruly behavior. When the case was eventually called before the court, the government attorney said because of the guardian's harassing and threatening behavior, she had requested a male colleague to accompany her. At this point, the guardian asked to approach the bench.

All the parties came forward, and the guardian began to reply loudly and forcefully to the government's complaints. As he spoke, his voice grew louder and louder, and then he began gesturing. His gestures and voice increased in magnitude, and soon he was screaming and pointing his finger at my face.

I tried to calm him down and said softly, "Counsel."

He ignored me, so I repeated it. And then once again, and again.

The transcript shows I asked him to calm down or said "Counsel" twenty-six times.

Finally, he stepped back and yelled, "Are you going to hold me in contempt? Go ahead, hold me in contempt."

Then he began to smugly cite all the court of appeals cases where lawyers had been held in contempt by the trial court and the appellate court had later reversed the lower court's decision.

"No," I said. "I'm not going to hold you in contempt. You're fired."

"You have no basis to take me off the case," he yelled.

"I'm removing you because you have been holding up court proceedings, and not once have you said or done anything to act in the child's best interests. Since that is the basis of your appointment, you are not serving it."

He went silent as he stared up at me in disbelief before noisily packing his briefcase and stomping out, yelling about how badly he had been discriminated against.

I apologized to the child and the parents for the unpleasant experience and appointed a new guardian *ad litem* for the child. The family was appreciative, especially the child. But this meant another delay, and more time waiting for resolution. Time seems so much longer for a child.

For children subjected to the legal system, it's crucial to hear the child's voice. Sometimes, children don't understand how bad their situation is because it is all they know. They get scared by the circumstances and the legal system. Fear raises its ugly head early in life.

The environment has improved in the family court to minimize the trauma of the experience. The décor and layout have been modified to create an ambiance of care and concern for the child. The waiting room contains books and games, and the case might be heard in a smaller, less intimidating, brightly decorated court-room. Kids are offered huggable toys to hold during a hearing.

The court was also divided into divisions: the Family Court, the Criminal Division, the Civil Division, the Probate Division, and so on. Judges were assigned to a division for a set period and then rotated to another. Although we refer to it as a rotation, it was not that at all. The chief judge made the assignments, but all were subject to change at any time. Adjustments were commonly made as judges retired and new ones came on board. Therefore, it was common for court assignments to be shuffled around to accommodate the new arrivals. Each assignment usually lasts for two years, but some were shorter. The change in assignments allowed individuals to concentrate on a single field and learn about it in depth. However, remaining too long on one assignment can become tedious. Switching assignments kept us motivated and interested as we absorbed the nuances of each area.

My time on the neglect calendar was due to end, but I found myself reassigned for another year. I panicked. My brain was telling me I'd had enough. To continue the work and remain impartial was going to be impossible.

While I loved the kids, I hadn't expected to experience so much emotional pain. Each case was heartbreaking, and I found it difficult to put my personal feelings to one side when deciding cases. Every day, I was exposed to the crippling damage caused by physical and emotional abuse and awful living conditions. It was so much worse than I could have imagined. I just couldn't stomach the thought of another year's exposure to this human misery.

I spoke with the chief judge who was responsible for assignments. I explained it was a privilege and an honor to work with the neglect cases, but it was damaging my psyche. I can still hear the children singing, "You Are My Sunshine" and visualize the little boy with chocolates spilling from his pockets. The images might swell your heart momentarily, but then reality bites and shatters it into tiny pieces. Enough. "I've got to go," I said tearfully.

The chief looked into my eyes and nodded quietly as he searched my face.

"No problem," he said knowingly, having suffered the same himself. "You've got to go."

He switched my assignment to a criminal calendar.

My first felony assignment presented me with the opportunity to preside over a jury trial. I had once been fortunate enough to sit on a jury, unusual for a lawyer, and the experience taught me a lot. Among other things, it taught me new respect for the jury's role. I was determined to let each jury member know how important their job was and to make them comfortable in their unaccustomed temporary environment.

One of the more serious trials lasted a month and involved four defendants. They were charged with raping a young man with a pole, subsequently causing his death. It was a hideous crime and extremely graphic. The jury was warned it was a difficult case and might take a long time.

With two government lawyers and six defense lawyers, the case dragged on for several weeks. As the evidence came out, two of the four boys were the most culpable. Two others had been with the group but had not done anything specific to harm the victim that was observed by any witnesses. One sad indictment of the case was not just the cruelty that affected the young man because he was different but also the fact none of the observers tried to intervene or stop the rape.

I worked hard to make the jury feel focused, comfortable and appreciated. This was a long, gruesome trial, and they were giving up parts of their busy lives to be part of it. The trial dragged on for so long that it appeared likely to clash with my planned vacation, for which I had purchased non-refundable airline tickets.

There is no way to control the length of jury deliberations. The jury began deliberating ... and deliberated ... and deliberated. The jury was never deadlocked, but they were thorough and cautious as they reviewed the evidence repeatedly. I had to leave before they had concluded their lengthy deliberations. I briefed a colleague on the trial issues and arranged for him to preside over the final portion of the deliberations.

The jury found two defendants guilty and exonerated the other two. When I returned, I received a thank-you card signed by all the jurors. I have never heard of it happening before or since. Additionally, I learned the jury had purchased a gift for my courtroom clerk. It was rewarding to know they felt good about their role in the legal system.

A young woman, a recent college graduate, sat before me in the courtroom. She had imbibed alcoholic beverages at a weekend brunch. She drove home, somewhat impaired, talking on her cell phone. She failed to realize the car in front of her had stopped and rammed into it. The car she hit had a fancy tire mounted underneath the rear window. When her car smashed into the tire, it was rammed into the rear passenger compartment, killing the young man sitting there. The young woman was devastated and insisted on pleading guilty. She also insisted on receiving a jail sentence. A plea deal was struck with the prosecutor, and a specific sentence was also agreed upon as part of the deal. The only thing remaining was to officially sentence the defendant.

At the time of the accident, the parents of the young man had been preparing to attend a celebration of the father's successful career. It was one of the happiest moments of their lives. As the father was dressing for the event, he answered the phone and learned of his son's death. Then he had to inform his wife.

The victim's family and friends wrote letters to me. Even though the sentence was predetermined, I read them all, over fifty of them. Through those heartbreaking texts, I came to know this young man. The funny and loving stories I read about him filled my heart.

I also received letters on behalf of the defendant. She had been working her first job teaching boating to children. She was well-loved in the community and by her family.

Sentencing in cases where there has been a death is one of the most difficult experiences for a judge. In many ways, it is a memorial service for the loved ones left behind. Inevitably, they fill up one side of the courtroom while the defendant's family sits on the other, which happened in this case. Family members came to support the defendant, and relatives came to support the family of the deceased.

The law requires victims or their families be allowed to tell their stories and explain how a crime has impacted their lives. Usually, this victim impact statement is in writing and submitted to all parties before the actual sentencing hearing, but victims can also make a public statement in court.

In this case, the deceased young man's father had traveled from overseas to appear in the courtroom. He brought with him a cadre of young people, friends of his late son. But his wife did not attend; he explained she could not bear the pain.

The father spoke movingly about his son. He gave some examples of his son's humor which had people stifling laughter through their tears. He also spoke about his son's stolen future and the dreams and aspirations he had shared with his family. The father's voice trembled with emotion. Except for some stifled sobs, the room was silent. The spectators were mesmerized as the heartbroken father spoke. He ended his statement by looking up at me with tear-rimmed eyes and saying wistfully, "I thought he was going to change the world."

On the other side of the courtroom sat the family of the defendant. They were also sobbing. They were good people who understood the loss. But they were crying for their child, too. There was no solace for either family. The pain in the room was so intense it weighed heavily on my shoulders.

After reading so many letters on behalf of both sides, my job, besides sentencing the defendant, was to find peace or comfort for both families, without offending one or the other. It was an awesome responsibility, yet one that can give each family some of the much-coveted closure they may seek at these times.

As someone who spent many days looking at the pain in my parents' eyes after my accident, I am aware of the effect of such tragedies on families. I always tried to say some words to ease the pain of the victim's family during these sentencings, while also respecting the pain of the defendant's family. In cases such as this, it was not unusual, even six months later, for me to wake up at night remembering the sentencing, still feeling the pain and tears of both families. I don't think those painful memories will ever go away.

This case was atypical because the deceased and the defendant were white and educated, but it made no difference to the tough sentencing.

Sadly, in most trials, both victims and defendants are non-white. Children are often killed during neighborhood quarrels, frequently over bad drug deals or battles over drug territory.

In one case, two male defendants in their early twenties approached the car of two other guys who had stopped to buy street drugs from a competitor. They fired gunshots into the car as if they were shooting fish in a barrel. The victims in the car had been seriously wounded; they survived but sustained permanent injuries. At the sentencing, the families of the victims sat on one side of the courtroom, and the friends and family of the defendants were on the other side across the aisle. The tension was thick as the prosecuting attorneys asked the court to sentence each defendant to over one hundred years in prison. The lawyers wanted the young men locked away — warehoused.

The victims and their families have a right to speak, but sometimes, the defendant's family also requests the opportunity to speak. The judge decides whether to allow this. The family usually wants to plead for their loved one. I have always granted their request to speak, even when at times I feared they would become overly angry or emotional. I wanted them to feel they had done all they could and that they had been heard.

In this case, the parents of one of the defendants arrived late, just in time to hear the prosecutor ask the court to sentence the defendants to sixty years in jail. Usually, the families' statements are heard before the final arguments and requests by the lawyers, but in this case, traffic problems caused the parents to arrive late. The defense requested the court take the unusual step of letting the parents speak just as the court was ready to pronounce the sentence.

The entire courtroom hushed into ghostly silence. You could cut the tension in the air with a knife. While I anticipated an overly emotional plea from the family at this point, I granted them the opportunity to speak. Their son was going to prison. They needed to feel they had done what they could for him, even if their words were emotional and upsetting.

The parents approached the microphone at the podium slowly and respectfully. They were composed and remarkably calm. They were dressed as professionals, in business clothes, and they still had overcoats on. They thanked me for the opportunity to speak. They were brief, genuine, and sincere and said they loved their son and believed there was good in him. With tearful eyes, the mom looked up and said, "I understand he must go to prison." Then added quietly, "Please don't warehouse my son."

Their son did receive a significant sentence, but nothing as serious as the government had requested. Twenty years later, he was released thanks to good behavior during incarceration and recognition of his youth at the time of the offense. I could see he was a man who had changed for the better. Now he had high hopes for a happy and productive life.

After several years in the Criminal Division, I moved to the Civil Division where I was responsible for cases involving car accidents and medical malpractice. Other cases involved issues such as lead poisoning and property disputes. As part of this assignment, we also spent several weeks in Landlord and Tenant court.

It was eye-opening to see images of apartments and the conditions some tenants were living in. I saw more photos of rats than I had ever seen in biology class. This demonstrated a dire need for affordable housing.

Next, I was assigned to juvenile/family court. The assignment covered cases involving children under the age of eighteen. Working with young people was a learning experience. The youngest child involved was about six years old, but because he was truly unable to grasp the legal concepts of a trial, his case was eventually dismissed.

I was often troubled by the law sometimes requiring the court to impose middle-class responsibilities and values on those who had not grown up with them. This was illustrated in Juvenile Court.

As a child, I had been brought up in a household with strict rules, curfews, and chores I sometimes found confining. Some of my cousins were nurtured in a far looser environment than mine, with no rules, no curfews, and no boundaries on their behavior. I was always envious of their carefree ways. When one of those cousins later informed me that she had been jealous of my up-bringing, I was shocked. She explained because I had to follow rules, I knew the boundaries of acceptable behavior as well as the consequences of misbehavior, so it was clear to me I was loved. Those rules, she said, gave a child a sense of security.

The youths appearing before me in Juvenile Court were not children who were gently awakened in the morning by their parents, fed a healthy meal, and dropped off at school. What I learned in court — from the kids, their lawyers, their families, and social workers — was these kids did not live the normal American life as we idealize it. These young people woke themselves up in the morning. They put on what clothing they could find easily and left the usually chaotic house without food. Occasionally, when they had a dollar or two, they purchased or stole snacks from a store before joining their friends at school. They would frequently sneak out of class and find a place to smoke marijuana, often behind the school building. It was rare to find a juvenile over ten years old who had not smoked marijuana. Additionally, it was popular to lace marijuana with PCP, a tranquilizer with a hallucinogenic effect. This did not make energetic and enthusiastic students, quite the opposite.

All this was not to say they were not loved, but perhaps they had some problem recognizing it, and escaping from their pain temporarily was therapeutic. Of course, they were also escaping from the violence in the neighborhood and the rage of poverty: the feeling of the unfairness in it all, the "Why me?" Without basic survival skills or a secure home, many were too afraid to go to school or even venture outside their neighborhood. They had seen people shot just getting on a bus or walking down a street. Many had held their friends as they died. All had been threatened at some time by somebody. Many lived with addicts, and all were terrified of the police.

To be frank, they were war victims, not from Syria or Yemen or other politically unstable conflict zones but from the United States of America, the land of the free.

I tried to empower young people to take control and change their lives. To give them a sense they had some control, I told them what the options were, what actions they could take, and what my response was for each. It was a form of William Glasser's Reality Therapy. Glasser believed in giving a person their options clearly and explaining the consequences of each choice. Then, fully informed, the person chooses.

I attempted to be as clear and transparent as possible, repeatedly informing them that their actions spoke louder than their words.

They were all surprisingly excellent advocates for themselves. They had developed street-savvy skills to survive in their war zone. Frequently, they shushed their lawyers and made their plea, and were often good. But they failed to follow it up with corrective action. I needed to see evidence they would *do* something, not just talk. This was not easy for them because it's almost impossible to persuade a young person to seek education when they remain convinced they are unlikely to live beyond twenty-five.

Their problems were also compounded. Even if a suitable education program could be found, transportation costs, lack of family support, or neighborhood conflicts predestined failure. Occasionally, the determined made it — but only with lots of luck.

I publicly acknowledged each positive step I saw them take; I told them how proud I was of them. When I asked them if they were proud of themselves, their shoulders went back, they straightened their stance, and with a slow smile, they said, "Yes."

"Don't let anyone take that from you," I told them.

My wheelchair confused them. Some of the young kids at one of the homeless shelters believed I made my home inside the courthouse, with living quarters behind the door at the back of the bench. They came to think of me as their grandmother. This was a tad disturbing to me until I realized some of their grandmothers were still in their late thirties and early forties. Some of these young adults were already parents; one fourteen-year-old had a girlfriend who was pregnant with his second child. He wanted to be better than his absent dad, but with no education or job skills, his future options seemed limited.

Many were surprised to learn they could achieve more than they realized and came to acknowledge following rules was cool.

"How hard was it to follow the rules and do it right?" I asked.

"It wasn't hard," they mumbled, usually with a shy smile.

"Duh," I replied with an answering grin.

A defendant who was doing well came into the courtroom one day, smiled at me, and told me all he had accomplished. I praised him, and I told them I was proud of him, but I said I hoped he was proud of himself. I urged him not to let anyone rob him of his self-dignity.

The Juvenile Court is a thermometer of a country's culture, education system, and social advancement. Parents—if they could be bothered, located, or sober enough—often accompanied the defendants to the table. Watching the interactions from my seat on the bench was often revealing. Frequently, a child made a rude remark or uttered a curse word, only to have the parent tell them to "shut their m*f* mouth" or something similar.

One mother complained her child did not respect her. I asked for an example. She said she gave her sixteen-year-old son two movie tickets and three hundred dollars to have a nice Valentine's Day with his girlfriend, yet he still cursed out his mom.

"You gave him what?" I asked.

"Three hundred dollars," she said.

"What did he do to earn it?" I asked.

"What?" she said.

"What did he do to earn it?" I repeated.

"Nothing," she said.

"Then you have taught him he does not have to respect you to get what he wants."

One case involved a fourteen-year-old who was angry with the world. I learned a lot about the rage of poverty from these kids. This young man had stolen a car and was chased by two police officers on bicycles, who intercepted him. The young man initially stopped the car, but then he stepped on the gas and knocked down one of the officers, nearly killing him.

The young man had a loving single mom, but she couldn't protect him from poverty, poor education, drugs, and crime in the only neighborhood they could afford to live in. An agreement was reached with all parties, and the young man agreed to move to a structured rehabilitation setting and receive a much-needed education.

The defendant was well represented by excellent court lawyers who documented his multiple learning disorders. Test results confirmed an extremely low IQ; he could not read or write and was physically impaired. On the day of sentencing, exceptions were made so the injured police officer, his boss, and his work friends could attend. The injured officer's wife was also present. Usually, no public spectators are permitted to attend juvenile hearings. The courtroom was charged with emotion. The young defendant made a remarkable speech. He apologized sincerely, and then he told the court what he was learning, how excited he was about life, and that he no longer had a death wish. He told them he was learning to read. This was followed by emotional testimony from the family and friends of the fallen officer, as well as lots of tears.

Then, the defendant's mother requested to speak. Although the victim has a right to give an impact statement, there is no such right embedded in the law for the defendant's family. It was important to let her speak. In a way, Mom was a victim, too, and I had learned personal tragedies go much further than ourselves. She needed to be heard, especially by her son, and he needed to feel his story was being heard, too. The atmosphere in the court-room intensified as the spectators expected to hear unpleasant things from her. She surprised us all.

She apologized for her son's behavior and said, "He was not raised that way and his behavior was so wrong." She asked what she could do to help with the healing, and she cried, telling the victims how sorry she was. She offered to work for the victim's family, and I recall promises of baked goods, too. She expressed her gratitude for the help her son had received and the changes he had been able to make with the court's support. She poured out her heart — not with bitterness or rancor, but with love and sincere gratitude. By the end of her speech, the tension in the room had melted, and everyone was hugging each other. The young man, feeling supported and loved, went on to do quite well. I later heard he even went on to establish a good relationship with the officer he had injured.

Recently, the Washington, D.C. City Council took a fresh look at the sentencing structure and its effects. They subsequently passed a law that took into consideration recent studies and re-search showing children's brains and thought processes are not fully mature until they are well into their twenties. I had wit-nessed this repeatedly. When I asked young men, "What were you thinking?" inevitably, they hung their heads and said, "I wasn't thinking." Which was the actual truth.

A new law has taken into account this lack of maturity. It allows defendants convicted of murder or attempted murder before they were twenty-five and have served a particular number of years in prison to file a motion seeking a reduction in sentence or even early release. The court considers ten factors in deciding whether to decrease or end a sentence. The details of the original offense are not the focus. More important is the defendants' discipline while incarcerated, their level of remorse, and their efforts toward rehabilitation.

One man had been convicted of murder just before the age of eighteen. Found guilty by a jury, he had been sentenced to sixty-five years in jail. He had now served twenty-two years and was only thirty-eight years old. He submitted a motion for a reduction in sentence.

The facts of the murder were horrendous, but now the defendant had the opportunity, upon reflection, to fill in any gaps he did not share at the time of the offense. He was also able to explain his background and how he had used his time while being incarcerated. This defendant had grown up without a positive male role model or a father. His mother was addicted to hard drugs and prostituted herself for drug money. As a small child, the defendant had watched his mother as she was assaulted and raped before his eyes. As he grew up in the D.C. community among the turf wars and neighborhood beefs, he had no protector, let alone a role model or mentor. Inevitably, he learned from the streets how to behave and what it meant to be a man. His duty was to protect himself and his family, particularly his mother.

One youth in the neighborhood did not like the defendant and attacked him whenever possible, on one occasion shooting him. The defendant tried to ignore him, but this was difficult because the neighborhoods were small and close. One day, the other man approached the defendant's mother in a field near their home. He put a gun to her head and said, "Tell your son I am coming for him." She raced home hysterically and scared. She told her son and then took more drugs.

The defendant decided the animosity had to end.

He called a friend, and they went to the home of the threatening man to see if they could clear the air. Once inside the home, they were talking when the victim appeared to be reaching for a gun. Since he had previously been shot by this man, the defendant reacted and shot first. He killed the man, who, he said, was a bully.

Most of this information had not come out at his trial. Consequently, it had been deemed a revenge killing, and hence the lengthy sentence. We had a new hearing to listen to the new evidence and consider the motion to reduce his sentence.

The defendant's mother testified. She confessed to her addiction and the horrible things her son had witnessed. She told about her experience in the field when the decedent had put the gun to her head and her response. After her son was sentenced, she learned she could not visit him in prison when using drugs.

This became her motivation to clean up, and she did. She quit drugs, took a job, and established regular communication with her son. Over the years he was incarcerated, they developed a deep understanding and a solid relationship. The defendant, despite the daunting stretch of sixty-five years behind bars hanging over him, did not give up. He took academic courses and earned a degree from an accredited college. He provided a list of books he had read during his incarceration. It was extensive and impressive. The victim's family attended the hearing and remarkably had no objections to the defendant's release.

So, after twenty-two years, he was released just in time to accept his diploma in person for his college degree. He continues to thrive in his community.

A mother arrived in the courtroom wearing a one-piece, skin-tight, silver outfit with a plunging neckline that encased her to the knees. She was young, beautiful, and voluptuous, so it was not just her knees grabbing everyone's attention. I even thought I heard a quiet gasp as she approached the inner well of the court. I was not sure if this was her daily wardrobe or if she had assumed the judge would be male, with sympathies to be swayed by her appearance.

Her son had been missing for days. He had disappeared from the youth home where he lived. Six years old, he suffered from serious learning and mental health disabilities. His mother, who had three other children, seemed unconcerned. She stated she was happy to take her son back if he wished to come home.

The boy had frequently run away from his youth home. Inevitably, he found his way back to his mother's home, only to be completely neglected there. It was a classic case of abandonment. Nobody wanted or loved him. He received no care or help with his learning disabilities. But as bad as it was, he preferred to be home. Perhaps it was the only place he felt he could survive, considering his limitations.

Case after case has demonstrated to me that children yearn to be trusted and are happy to soak up any praise, especially from a judge. Their parents, who have experienced deprivations growing up, inadvertently fail and deprive them of their innocence. Unfortunately, many of those parents don't even realize they are doing it; they simply treat their kids the same way they were treated. It's a harsh indictment of our civilized modern world when children repeat their parents' experiences of neglect.

Surprisingly, I have seen only a few of my juvenile defendants return as adult criminals. If they do return, they always recognize me. I encouraged them to request a different judge, but they declined, telling their lawyer, "She is a fair judge," Which means a lot to me.

Many adult defendants grew up in the system. Often, those who came before me had been in trouble as young people. I took from this that adults were just as hungry for love and praise as kids.

In the Misdemeanor Section, cases tend to be less serious, such as unlawful entry, drug possession, and shoplifting/theft. As a young prosecutor, these were my first criminal cases, but as a judge and now a person with broader life experiences, I take a different viewpoint as to why people commit these minor offenses.

Most defendants have a drug addiction, often brought on by mental health issues. Mental health issues carry a negative stigma;

however, frequently, the defendants won't seek help. They self-medicate instead, using street drugs. Phencyclidine (PCP) is one of the most popular, but its level of purity is always suspect.

When arrested and if incarcerated, defendants are given medications appropriate to their mental condition. But convincing them to continue taking the correct meds is tough, as it's asking them to admit their disturbed psyche is a permanent condition.

Many of the defendants are children of addicts who were using drugs at the time of conception and birth. They come into the world with damaged livers, impaired brains, and limited capability of receiving education or learning practical skills. Whereas many of us define ourselves by our jobs and what we do, the less fortunate among us are not able to achieve such status and often struggle to discover a sense of self.

I ask them if they want help. Sometimes, their lawyers will not let them answer. If they do reply, they are usually hesitant to say yes. They wonder, *what if I fail?* Or worse, *what if I make it?* Their entire world could change with either choice. I ask them to consider accepting treatment and tell them, "You are worth it. You matter. You deserve a happy and healthy life. I am here to fight for you, but I can't do it without you."

Often, they cry when they hear that and tell me no one had ever spoken to them so considerately.

One man who had a tough time on probation asked me for one more chance. I looked at my notes and counted all his previous chances and what I had asked of him each time. It's sometimes difficult to convince a defendant playing by the rules can make their life easier. I had tried simple things like "Follow your curfew for a few weeks and come back successful," but he could never do it. This was his tenth hearing. As he pleaded for one more chance, I asked him how it might be different this time and when the pattern would end.

He couldn't answer.

"I'm sorry," I said. "At some point, you must realize if you refuse to be responsible for your actions, there will be consequences. There are no more chances left." I then revoked his probation and imposed the sentence. As the marshal approached to take him to the cellblock, he looked up at me and said, to my surprise, "It's okay, Judge. You have been fair, and you cared. Thank you."

One eighteen-year-old young woman consistently missed her court dates. Her original charge was assault, but each time she failed to turn up, a new warrant was issued. She was arrested and charged with failing to appear in court. She was getting more cases charged against her simply by failing to show up and deal with the original one. When she came before me for the umpteenth time, it was clear she had serious mental health issues but preferred street drugs to a medical routine. On this occasion, she, too, had gotten to the place where there could be no more chances. She began crying and describing her difficult life. She said people laughed at her and cursed and threatened her because of her looks, and it was all unfair. I agreed with her and told her I was sorry that was her experience, but acting out in anger was not the solution. She said she understood. Then, after a pause, she said, "Can I go home now?"

"No," I said. "Not today."

She screamed and cursed. As the marshals dragged her to the cellblock, she yelled, "Mother****, bitch and disabled, too."

I looked at her with a smile and said, "Is that supposed to be news?"

She returned the next day to finish the hearing. After some obvious whispered coaching by her lawyer, she contritely apologized. But when she was not released, her temper flared again in another angry outburst. She was sent for a forensic exam, and medication was again recommended. The cycle continued.

One man had a bad habit of assaulting people on the street. He was homeless, and it was clear he had mental health issues, in addition to his drug use. A forensic exam was done, and he was deemed incompetent and in need of residential hospital-ization and treatment. The case continued for thirty days. When he returned, he tried to convince me he was now fit and well, or what we legally refer to as competent. At his court appearance, he told me about the titanium in his neck and offered to show me his x-rays. I looked at what he had brought, and I listened to his lawyers, but it was clear he was not back to a legal status of com-petency. Indeed, the doctors recommended more hospitalization. The defendant's case was reviewed every four weeks, and each time, he arrived with his x-rays and explained about the titanium in his neck. He was chatty, and I found him quite delightful to converse with. Finally, one day, he came into the courtroom via the cellblock, looked up at me, and began yelling spontaneously and excitedly.

"Judge," he yelled, "I'm competent, I'm competent. You must let me out."

Sure enough, the doctors had finally opined he was legally competent.

"Well, sir," I said. "Today, we are going to discuss this."

"You have to let me out," he said. "The jail can't handle me."

"Why?" I said.

"It's because of my health," he said. "Judge, it's the titanium in my neck. I'm one-third paralyzed."

"One-third?" I said. "How does that work?"

"Well," he said, "because of the titanium in my neck, I can't move my head from side to side." As he explained this, he turned his head easily from side to side. "I have my x-rays. Do you want to see them?"

The defendant repeated himself over and over, chattering excitedly.

Finally, I had to interrupt. "Sir, I've seen your x-rays, remember them well, and have been listening to you carefully, but now it is my turn to talk, okay?"

The defendant stopped, took a breath, and in great earnest said, "I am sorry, Judge. It's your turn to talk. I am excited, but I'm just old and paralyzed like you."

There was a collective gasp in the courtroom at his last remark. I spotted the defense attorney looking at the floor as if seeking a place to escape. I turned, put my hand on my hip, and said to the defendant, "Who told you I was *old?*"

The people in the courtroom laughed. The defendant quickly apologized and said, "I'm the only old one, Judge." He was released later the same day and promised to take all his prescribed medications. He had already served as much time as his original crime allowed, so with restored health there was no legal basis to continue holding him. I hope he lives a better life now.

It never ceases to amaze me when someone points to my physical condition and others become embarrassed. Do they think it's something I am not aware of or can ignore? It is right there to be seen. The elephant is in the room.

I tend not to ignore elephants, but I don't dwell on them either. I'm also not afraid to use them if the opportunity presents itself.

When defendants claim that they don't want to take their medications because they are laughed at or some unusual physical attribute makes them feel uncomfortable or ashamed, I find it useful to quote Lady Gaga's self-acceptance lyrics from her song "Born This Way."

The reference never fails to raise a smile or renew interest in what has often become tedious proceedings. I tell them to be proud because they are born this way, and it's exactly who they were meant to be. Coming from a judge in a wheelchair, it seems to grab their attention.

One of the greatest rewards for a judge is when an active drug addict becomes a recovering addict. Then, they are filled with pride, dress differently, and behave with dignity. Even if the recovery doesn't endure, they have felt and known it, and judges can be the catalyst to make it happen.

Some make a point of coming back to tell me. Others say no one told them they were worth it before, and it made an enormous difference to their confidence.

As a person of Irish-German heritage, I was not raised in a touchy-feely environment. But my accident taught me the value of telling people how you feel and trying to be aware of how they are feeling. Many of the people who come before me are simply seeking love, dignity, and some affirmation. However, they don't know how or where to find it and are overwhelmed by life and what the court system demands of them. They cannot apply for jobs because they have no birth certificate, no social security number, and no funds to obtain them. Some agencies help with funding for documents but not transportation.

When you have no fixed address, or you are couch-surfing with family or friends, applying for any job or document is difficult. Occasionally, I tell defendants it's okay to ask for help. I say, "If your ship doesn't dock, you have to swim out to meet it." One defense attorney told me his client's response had been, "But I can't swim."

Despite these impossible situations, they survive. I tell them, "Look how strong you are. You are still here."

Frequently, a judge's comments on the bench carry extra weight. In today's parlance, we are influencers. Very few people are hardened, remorseless criminals. The majority who come before us endure difficult personal lives that drive them to illegal acts, mostly to survive. The state, via the judge, recognizes and hears their pain, even if sometimes the outcome results in the temporary loss of their liberty.

None of us can put ourselves in their place or intimately know the road leading them to the courtroom. But whatever the outcome, the judge must never, especially when sentencing, take away the defendant's dignity. People remember the words you use to speak to them.

In the Universal Declaration of **Human Rights**, Article One states, "All **human** beings are born free and equal in **dignity** and **rights**." Respect is always appreciated. Take it away, and we are destroyed.

As a judge, one of my more pleasurable tasks is marrying people. Some couples make special arrangements with a particular judge to officiate their ceremony. Others take potluck.

Some of the most memorable weddings I officiated were the first same-sex marriages after they were approved by the City Council in D.C. Many of the couples had been together for many years in stable relationships. Being officially recognized by the law, accepted, and approved by society finally gave their relationship approval and dignity. The joy of those couples was particularly touching and added pleasing warmth and color to the typically bland courthouse wedding. One couple had been together for over twenty years. They came to D.C. from another jurisdiction that did not recognize their partnership in legal terms. The relief and the tears came spontaneously, and they expressed disbelief they were truly, finally married. When I asked another same-sex couple, "Are you ready?" they answered quickly, "We've been ready for twelve years." After the ceremony, many of these couples thank me for being willing to do the service. But it is a true gift to me to be able to preside over such wonderful unions.

My greatest joy, though, was to officiate over the weddings of some of my former staff members and law clerks.

SKIING

My travel companion and friend, Carlos, approached me at work with a proposal. He explained he had just returned from a ski trip in New Mexico. While there, he noticed people skiing in what looked like a sit-down ski accompanied by another stand-up skier. But what truly grabbed his attention was those skiers were allowed to go directly to the front of the lift line. His proposal: You learn to ski, and I will be your ski buddy, and we can skip to the front of all the lift lines.

Carlos was serious about this idea. He thought it was just the kind of crazy thing I might enjoy. After some research, I learned a clinic in adaptive skiing was scheduled at a nearby ski hill. I signed up for both of us.

On the day of the clinic, it was pouring rain, but there was still snow on the ground. The undaunted ski instructors set us up in our skis—me on the monoski—wrapped us in plastic bags to protect us from the rain, secured the bags with duct tape, and headed to the slope.

I tried skiing once or twice back in my youth when I was still able to walk, but it was a disaster both times because I am not athletically inclined. In my early years, after observing me in ballet class, my parents encouraged me to try playing the flute instead.

I had never even seen a monoski. Now, I was about to be placed in this weird contraption to hurtle down hills at death-defying speed. Yikes.

A monoski is exactly what it sounds like —one single ski. I sat on the seat mounted on top, legs outstretched and knees hiked a bit. My feet were belted down into a protective casing. Then the rest of me was strapped tightly to the seat from chest to feet, which was unnerving. In response to my negative comments, the teachers proclaimed, "We have to bind you up to set you free."

Once secure in the seat, I grasped a pair of outriggers, one in each hand. The outrigger is a ski pole with a small ski on the bottom. Getting me aboard the chairlift required my assistant to grab the back of the seat portion of the monoski and raise it, allowing the chairlift to swing in and scoop up the monoski from behind, with a bit of extra lifting and pushing by the attendants. My assistant secured me to the lift chair with bungee cords, and we were whisked to the top of the slope. To disembark at the top of the mountain, I had to extend the outriggers in front of me and try to thrust my body forward.

Getting on and off the ski lift was daunting. As I rode up the mountain, the monoski was tilted a bit forward on the lift seat, due to the depth of the back of the monoski's seat. Once I'd settled down, I surveyed the scene far below. I couldn't look, so closed my eyes and tried to recall if I was religious or not.

During the early descents, the instructors held the back of the monoski and skied me down the beginner slope. Once I had achieved a sense of balance (neither an easy nor quick ac-complishment), the instructors attached tethers to the back of the monoski. Using the tether, the instructor, skiing behind me, controlled my speed and guided me on the turns.

The clinic was a four-day event. The first two-and-a-half days were drenching rain, bitter weather, and lots of falling to the ground, getting picked up, and falling over again. It was not fun. I was sitting in the lodge looking gloomy one day when one of the instructors asked me what was wrong. I explained that falling repeatedly in the cold rain was not particularly fun. Deciding I needed an attitude change, the instructor found an available monoski, tucked me in, tightened the straps, and took me out for some fun.

We rode the lift to one of the higher slopes. Just riding the lift did me in. When we dismounted, we turned downhill. From my low-seated position, I could only see a stretch of about three feet of snow and then a sudden drop. I had no idea what was on the other side. Was it three or thirty feet? I was overwhelmed with fear and panic. It left me speechless (a rare thing indeed). "We can't go down there," I squeaked. My instructor grinned and, as he shoved me over the edge, said, "Sure, we can." We were off, hurtling downhill at what seemed like an impossible speed.

The instructor held the monoski from behind, essentially skiing it for me. He began making turns, adjusting our speed, and dancing down the hill. I realized he was entirely capable of handling the situation and began to relax. I loved the speed. At times, we hit little mounds of snow, causing me to bump up and down in the ski, seeing double as it zoomed along. I grinned and laughed, interspersed with brief periods of alarm and terror, as we hurtled down the slope.

When we arrived at the bottom, I was exhausted from both the physical and emotional effort, but I beamed a huge smile. Back inside the lodge, some of the instructors asked if I had enjoyed my ride. I grinned from ear to ear and admitted I loved it. The instructor who had driven me down the hill looked at his colleagues, smiled slowly, and said simply, "She's hooked."

Since then, I have skied every winter. My friends join me, and I am truly incorporated into the sports world. I always have an instructor and a buddy along, so I end up skiing with an entourage. The companions perfectly enhance the experience. When I ski, I feel free, normal, and at peace with the world. Gliding down a long, wide slope and seeing the blue sky against the mountainous horizon is a humbling experience, a reminder of our insignificant place in a massive world.

I now use a bi-ski. A bi-skier sits in a molded fiberglass shell above two specially designed skis. The two skis give a wider base and better balance than a monoski. I still like a tether to my instructor — it's purely a confidence thing — but I have skied steep terrain and always go fast. I love to hit the bumps and bounce till I see double, and I still grin from ear to ear by the time I reach the bottom of the hill. I get a kick out of having ski conversations in public places and watching people's reactions to the concept that a paraplegic can ski.

I haven't by any means perfected the sport — in fact, I consider myself the queen of crash and burn. I've suffered black eyes, a dislocated collar bone, bruises everywhere, and some minor concussions (now, I always wear a helmet), but I hope to keep skiing for as long as I can.

HELP FROM STRANGERS

As a person in a wheelchair, I attract foolish and occasionally bizarre comments.

While working at the Treasury Department, I was dressed professionally, carrying documents, and waiting for the elevator. As I entered, one passenger was looking for the correct button to push for her floor. She looked toward me and said, "So, a car accident?"

"Well, yes," I said. "But I thought you might say hello first." The woman turned away and remained silent.

Another time, a woman chased me to the elevator, yelling. When I turned around, she stopped shouting and said, "Oh, sorry. I thought you were someone else."

"Don't worry," I said, "we all look alike."

Most of these people are truly trying to be kind. I've lost count of the number of times I've been wheeling along nicely at a good pace when someone will interrupt whatever they are doing, risk life and limb dashing across a busy road, and stop me to ask if I need help.

I'm often tempted to inquire, "Why? Wasn't I going fast enough?"

Frequently, people enter the elevator and seeing me seated there ask, "Can I push the button for your floor?" assuming I have been going up and down for hours waiting for someone to help because I can't push a button on my own.

Sometimes, people just want to say something nice. One day, a couple stopped me and my friends to say that looking at us made them see "true love and tenderness." We were merely waiting in line for an event.

A fellow student once pointed to my wheelchair and said, "Are you paralyzed, or is it psychosomatic?" I had no idea how to answer.

Another regular chuckle-maker is when I ask someone if a place is accessible for me, and they answer, "Oh, yes. There are only one or two steps." Which, for me, may as well be the Great Wall of China.

I recognize people are good at heart. And while these experiences are sometimes irritating, they are driven by someone caring about or acknowledging my situation.

At the courthouse during one of my jury trials, some police witnesses saw me pushing on a wall as I pivoted off it, around a corner. By the time I arrived back at my office, they had stuck a traffic ticket on my door for "Failure to yield right of way." They had a good laugh.

Once, I was alone in Paris and wanted to cross the road. It was before the age of curb cuts, so I had to turn around and reverse down the curb while leaning forward. Then I scooted across the street. But remounting the curb was something I couldn't do alone, and all the pedestrians were studiously ignoring me. "*S'il vous plait?*" I said loudly, looking around. Those who had been feigning total indifference came alive with concern and sprinted over to help, four of them, one to each wheel. As they lifted me, I noticed others nearby who were pretending not to look but hesitating until they were sure I was safely underway. I spotted sly grins of encouragement.

My wheelchair has forced me to sit patiently, look, and try to understand the people I pass or meet. Their eyes are the windows to their soul. One can read fear, shame, passion, pride, tolerance, bigotry, understanding, or misunderstanding.

I have learned it is me, not the observer, who decides who I am.

In a way, my disability has been a rare gift. There is a strange beauty and comfort in it all. It's not without inconveniences, but it also has advantages. (For example, I'm frequently pushed to the front of the line, and from my height perspective, I'm the first to notice if a woman is pregnant.) At times, I'm treated as if I am invisible, but invisibility allows me to listen, observe, and learn.

My life experience has enriched me and made me wiser, and I want to share this good fortune with others. I try to do that at work and in my personal life. At work, I listen to and carefully watch every defendant or plaintiff in the courtroom. Everyone is a special and unique person with their own needs, talents, and ways of expressing them. My job is to understand them and then work with the facts at hand.

I have had the privilege of touching people's lives and hopefully making a positive difference. I have been moved by how different we all are and how much we have in common. I feel so blessed to be alive and different.

When I meet an inconsiderate person, I chuckle and remind myself they are merely another TAB (temporarily able-bodied) person trying to do their best. I smile with some condescension. I used to be one of them.

Then, I look for the next adventure. Because, to me, each day is a grand adventure.

If you relax and go with it, this wheelchair life confers some advantages. For example, you can use the big stall in the public bathroom without feeling guilty. You can get half-price tickets and transportation discounts in many cities. You can board the airplane first (though, unfortunately, you get off last), and there is always someone to escort you when you get off the plane. You can get away with extra carry-on luggage (by claiming it is medical supplies, which it usually is). You can skip to the front of the line at national monuments and ride the roller coaster two times in a row. You can frequently get a good parking space, and downhills are always a cheap thrill — you don't even need snow.

More importantly, you get the benefit of people's kindness and their desire to share life with you. Once people see you can go with the flow joyfully, they find adventures to share with you. Friends have given me piggyback rides through the Batu Caves of Malaysia and the Acropolis in Athens. They have tied me to their motorcycles with bungee cords and taken me for a spin, let me co-fly their airplanes, and introduced me to aerobatics. (I loved the double wingovers and upside-down flying.) I've sailed the Swedish seas, danced till I flipped over backward, and waterskied on glassy lakes. When I careen down a snowy mountain on my bi-ski and then ease myself into my wheelchair, the pitying looks disappear.

EPILOGUE

No one could have convinced me on September 3, 1970, the day the car flipped, that my life would turn out so full of joy. I have had the honor and privilege of serving my country as a judge and making a difference in people's lives. I regularly attend theater, ski, play my flute, and travel. I have marveled at amazing sights and relished meeting extraordinary people. I treasure my law clerk family and many other amazing friends. My life is sweet. I am at peace each day, even just sitting on my balcony with my view of the Washington Monument and the Lincoln Memorial.

Friends, family, coworkers, and strangers have opened their arms and their hearts to show me the good in life. That is the best part of each of those experiences, and it has made my life rich. I am surrounded by family and friends who are willing to tolerate my idiosyncrasies. (Some even like me.) I have a brand-new blue car, live in a beautiful condominium, and am happier than I could have ever imagined — even in my wildest dreams. Being different has opened and expanded my world to the extent I have become so accustomed to it that I now feel completely at ease in my skin.

But a recent event one day in court did give me a bit of a jolt.

As I wheeled onto the bench, the clerk, as usual, announced, "Everyone, please rise if you can."

I was surprised when a pretty young woman at the end of the first row failed to comply with this long-standing custom, marking respect for the law. Even more astonishing, she was grinning an inane but happy smile. I thought this curious, so I leaned over and softly asked the courtroom clerk why she was grinning but not standing. He put his hand in front of his face to disguise his laughter.

"Judge, she is in a wheelchair," he said, his eyes laughing.

It was a full-circle moment.

She was a student attorney thrilled to see a person in a wheelchair could succeed and be respected in a legal career. I was honored to be that person.

MY TEAM

Judges rely on the work of their team. The practice of law is a complex matter which can have serious implications for people's lives. To avoid misunderstandings or unjust decisions, judges must interpret evidence, facts, and written and spoken words. One of the more pleasurable aspects of my job has been debating the twists and turns of cases with my clerks and my team. I have had the good fortune to work with nineteen law clerks. They have made a memorable contribution to my life and career I will always treasure. I'm honored to share a few of their anecdotes here.

Jeremy

"Shall we begin?" said the judge.

The prosecuting attorney was a tall, middle-aged man in a smart suit. "The defendant," he said, "failed to turn up at a meeting with her social worker as directed by a recent court order. I have the confirmation of nonattendance from the social worker here, Your Honor."

The court clerk motioned him to step forward and read out the document he was holding. It confirmed the defendant's failure to report.

The judge turned toward the defense, glared at them with an appropriate judicial stare, and said, "Does your client offer any explanation for not attending?"

The defendant's lawyer hesitated before answering. During the pause, his client answered for him.

"I had a car accident," she said in a shaky but loud voice while remaining seated.

"Were you injured?" said Pat, not wishing to inflame matters more by raising matters about proper court procedure.

"Yes," she said. "I've been unable to work."

"But you can still walk," said Pat.

"Yes, but who are you to be judging me? How could you, in your privileged position, know what it's like to struggle and be mobility-impaired?"

The courtroom gasped.

Pat remained calm and said, "Could you come to the side of the bench, please."

As the woman slowly approached, I could see the shock in her eyes as she noticed the wheelchair ramp and lift to the side of the bench.

Pat wheeled over to her and said quietly, "I never make excuses, and I won't accept anything less from you."

Liz

Two incidents right at the beginning of my clerkship were terrifying. One, when I laughed in the courtroom behind the clerk's half-partition with the courtroom clerk after the hearing was over. The other was when I laughed in the courtroom with Cynthia, her secretary at the time. Both times Pat barked at me. I couldn't even see her, but boy could I hear her.

She explained later that the courtroom is usually for people facing one of the worst moments of their life. Pat did not want that diminished or disrespected by the sound of people laughing at inappropriate times.

Karen

Pat once told me she can't stand being told she's an "inspiration." Well, like it or not, she is stuck with it. Because she is. Pat is genuine, compassionate, hard-driving, caring, curious, and hilarious. She loves people, knows how to embrace challenges and change, adores art, ideas, and culture, and has seen more of this world than anyone I know.

She listens and makes time for the people she cares about. She brings people together. She will have you over for Thanksgiving. She will tell you what you need to hear, even if you don't necessarily want to hear it. She will tell you when she sees a problem, but not without offering a shoulder to lean on or an idea to help fix it in the same breath.

Pat will send you a greeting card in the mail or a hilarious meme (because yes, she knows what a meme is) just to say hello. Pat is feisty, saucy, and strong. And the fact she is these things, the fact she does these things would make any person remarkable. Pat is remarkable because of who she is and how she shows up for others.

But it's foolish to pretend there is not another layer to this, a layer adding a depth of challenge and richness I, indeed most, can never fully understand. Pat does all of this and does "life" as a woman in a wheelchair.

Pat has been a warrior and a champion for so many things, big and small, and perhaps not always by choice — simply by being a successful, honest, and generally badass human being who also uses a wheelchair in this world. Whether she likes it or not, many human beings might see her as an "inspiration."

But, for my part, I'll just start with the time she taught me it was okay to tie my shoes with my teeth.

I first met Pat when I began clerking for her in 2012, right after I graduated from law school at the University of Georgia. A former professor and mentor had put me in touch with Christina for coffee while I was job hunting. Christina was a few years out of law school and seemed sharp, in a smart kind of way, direct, and friendly. She told me Pat was wonderful, and if I was going to try to work for her, I should be aware she also did not suffer fools. Pat wanted a clerk to speak her mind and give feedback, even if a clerk disagreed with her. She told me clerking for Pat was an honor, and if I could do it, I absolutely should. I'm pretty sure I applied the next day. And then I followed up the day after. And the day after.

Several years after my clerkship ended, I suffered a bad bicycle accident. I broke parts of both arms, my left elbow, and my right wrist, and bruised my right foot so badly that I had trouble walking. I had to figure out quickly how to navigate each day, from getting dressed to spooning food into my mouth. Thankfully, my mom was able to fly to D.C. for the first few weeks to help. But it was Pat who picked up my mom from the airport.

After my mom left, Pat stayed in touch, and she checked on me. She helped me see, and eventually marvel at, how adaptable we humans can be when physical abilities, things we once took for granted, are suddenly taken away from us. I told Pat about how I learned to use my toes, teeth, random basket contraptions I was able to hang around my neck to carry things around the house, you name it. And Pat got it. She helped me see the other side of my injuries and learn to use my body and my mind in ways I never expected. And yes, at one point, she told me it was even okay to tie my shoes with my teeth because who cared how in the heck you got the job done, as long as the shoes got on your feet. And for that advice, I will always be grateful.

That's Pat. She can turn a blooper into an opportunity for some-thing fun and something better. And her ability to pivot, make a choice, and say or do the right thing is amazing. It's what sets her apart as a special person and a judge.

Nicky

As a prosecutor, Pat didn't keep track of wins and losses. To her, they were neither. If a defendant was found guilty, it was because the government had met its burden and proven its case beyond a reasonable doubt. If the defendant was acquitted, it was because the government had failed to meet its burden. Either way, it was justice, and either way, it was a win.

Only after working as a prosecutor myself did I realize how amazing it is Judge Broderick can put justice above her ego. As a prosecutor, it is so tempting to feel like each case reflects your skill as an attorney and lose sight of the fact justice is not served when an innocent person goes to jail or prison, even if your closing argument was outstanding. Judge Broderick taught me not to lose sight of this important fact, and although I frequently failed, I was a fairer prosecutor because of the time I spent with her.

Pat did not let her ego and pride control her actions. What mattered to her was justice being served in that case, even if it meant her decision was later overturned.

ABOUT THE AUTHOR

Patricia A. Broderick (Pat) was born in New York City and graduated from high school in New Jersey. She volunteered during a college summer in Guayaquil, Ecuador, as a social worker for the Meals for Millions Program. Pat received her BA in sociology *cum laude* from Trinity College in Washington, D.C., in 1971 and her master's degree in Rehabilitation Counseling from George Washington University in 1974. From 1974 to 1978, she served as a probation and parole officer for the Commonwealth of Virginia.

Pat studied law at The Columbus School of Law of The Catholic University of America. After passing the bar, she served as law clerk to the Honorable Henry F. Greene from 1981–2. In 1982, she was hired as an assistant U.S. attorney, and she was honored for her work in that role with the Department of Justice Special Achievement Award in 1988.

In 1989, Pat joined the Money Laundering and Asset Forfeiture Sections of the U.S. Department of Justice, where she won a second Special Achievement Award. In 1992, she was promoted to the Office of Financial Enforcement at the U.S. Department of Treasury to serve as chief of the International Section. She led the U.S. negotiating team for a bilateral Money Laundering Information Exchange Agreement with Paraguay and headed inter-agency assessment teams in Ecuador and Guatemala. Pat has lectured internationally on anti-money laundering methods in Panama, Belize, Martinique, Chile, and Malaysia. Beginning in

1994, she served as an attorney for the Task Force on Tax Refund Fraud. From 1995 to 1998, Pat served as special counsel to the Violence Against Women Office at the U.S. Department of Justice.

Pat was sworn in as an associate judge of the Superior Court of the District of Columbia in 1998, where she worked across several legal disciplines. In 2020, Judge Broderick was awarded senior status and is currently assigned to the Criminal Division.

Pat has taught trial advocacy at the George Washington University Law School and trial techniques at the Harvard University and the Emory University law schools. She has mentored at her alma maters, Trinity College, and The Columbus School of Law. In her leisure time, Judge Broderick enjoys the theater, traveling, and playing the flute, and she seizes every opportunity to ski.

Judge Broderick is a member of the National Association of Women Judges as well as its sister association, the International Association of Women Judges (IAWJ). In 2021, Judge Broderick spoke at the IAWJ Biennial Conference in Auckland, New Zealand, on "Diversity and Disability." She was listed in *Who's Who in American Women* in 1981.

ABOUT THE COLLABORATOR

Originally from London, England, Paul S. Bradley (pen name) sold his design company and retired. He has lived in Nerja, Spain since 1992, where he established a marketing agency to help Spanish businesses sharpen their communications to the rapidly growing number of foreign visitors. He's traveled extensively around the Iberian Peninsula visiting most of the ancient cities.

In the early years, he published lifestyle and property magazines, guidebooks, and travelogues in English, German, and Spanish before writing his first novel of the *Andalusian Mystery Series* which draws on his travel experiences, and as a volunteer translator in hospitals and police stations. The fifth volume of the series was self-published in 2022.

More recently, groups of discerning Alumni of Americans and Canadians have enjoyed his tour director's services. He's lectured about living in Spain and bullfighting and has appeared on local radio and TV.

Printed in the USA
CPSIA information can be obtained
at www.ICGtesting.com
LVHW022029130624
783028LV00007B/158/J

9 781950 544486